The 24-Hour Novel with ChatGPT

Andrew Parry

Published by Andrew Parry, 2025.

THE 24-HOUR NOVEL WITH CHATGPT

First edition. March 22, 2025.

ISBN: 979-8230073659

Written by Andrew Parry.

Table of Contents

The One-Day Challenge: Why it's Possible with ChatGPT 1

Getting Your Mind in Gear before You Begin 3

How to Ask ChatGPT for Original and Unique Story Ideas 5

Finding the Genre That Excites You 7

Starting with the End: Why Backward Thinking Works 9

Crafting a Powerful Climax before Anything Else 11

Building Your Story Backwards to the Beginning 13

Creating a Plot That Pulls Readers Forward 15

Outlining a Whole Novel in Under an Hour 17

Using ChatGPT to Flesh out a Three-Act Structure 19

Developing a Believable and Memorable Protagonist 21

Writing an Antagonist Readers Will Love to Hate 23

How to Build a Supporting Cast That Matters 25

Mapping Out Character Arcs with AI 27

Dialogue That Sounds Real and Feels Right 29

Giving Each Character a Unique Voice 31

How to Use ChatGPT to Write Show-Stopping Scenes 33

The Art of Scene Transitions with AI Assistance 35

Using ChatGPT to Set the Mood and Atmosphere 37

Crafting Settings That Feel Like Characters 39

Worldbuilding in Minutes with Prompts 41

How to Keep Your Story's Pacing Tight 43

Injecting Tension and Conflict with Every Chapter 45

Writing Emotional Beats That Resonate 47

ChatGPT and the Hero's Journey 49

Using ChatGPT for Theme Exploration and Consistency 51

How to Handle Flashbacks and Time Jumps with Style 53

Weaving Subplots without Losing Focus 55
Planting Setups and Delivering Payoffs 57
Writing a Gripping Opening Scene 59
Midpoint Twists That Reshape the Whole Story 61
Creating Cliffhangers That Beg for More 63
Writing a Satisfying Ending That Delivers 65
Revising and Editing with ChatGPT in Real Time 67
Self-Critiquing Your AI-Written Work 69
Getting the Tone and Voice Right from the Start 71
Writing in Different Tenses and Points of View with Ease 73
Using ChatGPT for Internal Monologues and Deep Thoughts 75
Keeping Your Story Cohesive in a Rush 77
Using Images to Inspire Writing Prompts 79
How to Use ChatGPT to Mirror Your Personal Style 81
Mixing Genres and Making It Work 83
Writing Fiction That Feels Autobiographical 85
Adding Symbolism and Metaphor with Subtlety 87
Collaborating with ChatGPT Like a Writing Partner 89
How to Direct and Refine AI Output 91
Turning AI-Generated Text into Your Own Voice 93
Avoiding Clichés and Creating Something Fresh 95
Writing for a Specific Audience with AI 97
Using ChatGPT for Research and Facts in Fiction 99
Maintaining Creative Control While Using AI 101
The Role of Intuition in One-Day Writing 103
Staying Motivated and Focused for a Marathon Session 105
What to Do When You Hit a Creative Block 107
Testing the Flow: Reading Aloud as You Write 109

Turning Your AI-Written Book into a Publishable Manuscript 111

How to Format and Export Your Final Draft 113

Cover Design and Titles with AI Input 115

Getting Feedback and Making Adjustments 117

The Joy of Finishing a Fiction Book in One Day 119

Prompting Like a Pro – Getting the Best Responses from ChatGPT 121

Creating Prompts That Enhance and Continue Your Story 124

The One-Day Challenge: Why it's Possible with ChatGPT

Writing a fiction book in a single day might sound like one of those wild, clickbait challenges that makes you roll your eyes and scroll on by. But stick around for a moment, because not only is it possible, it's actually a thrilling creative experience—especially when you're working with ChatGPT as your writing partner. The secret isn't about speed-typing until your fingers bleed. It's about working smart, staying focused, and using a tool like ChatGPT to remove the friction from the process of storytelling. Once you get into the flow of it, writing a full fiction book in a day becomes less of a gimmick and more of a game-changing creative strategy.

The first hurdle in writing any novel is the idea generation phase. This is where most people get stuck—staring at a blank screen, waiting for inspiration to drop from the ceiling like a spider. But ChatGPT doesn't need to wait for a muse. You can start a conversation, toss in a few words or a vibe you're curious about, and it will serve you a buffet of possible plots, themes, characters, and genres. Want a sci-fi thriller about time-traveling botanists? Or a psychological mystery set inside a dreamscape? Just ask. Within minutes, you can have ten solid ideas to choose from. That alone could take days or even weeks of brainstorming without AI.

Once you've picked your idea, the next roadblock in traditional writing is structure. Writers often wander aimlessly through their story, trying to discover the plot as they go. That's romantic and all, but not when you're trying to finish a book today. With ChatGPT, you can generate a solid three-act structure or hero's journey framework on demand. You can ask for a detailed chapter outline, subplots, scene breakdowns, or emotional beats, and suddenly what felt like a mountain becomes a mapped-out path. You don't have to guess where the story is going—because now you can plan it before your first sentence hits the page.

Another huge reason this is all possible in a day is because writing with ChatGPT eliminates the stop-and-start rhythm of solo drafting. You're not losing hours to indecision about what comes next or agonizing over sentence structure. You're in constant momentum. As soon as you finish one scene or chapter, you can ask ChatGPT for what's next, what to deepen, what to describe, or how to make the moment hit harder. It's like having a co-writer who never runs out of energy, never needs coffee breaks, and who can type as fast as you can think.

Now, let's talk length. When we say "fiction book," we're not necessarily talking about an 800-page fantasy tome with six points of view and a map at the front. This one-day writing method is best suited to novellas, short novels, or even full-length novels if you're in the zone and hyper-focused. Think 15,000 to 30,000 words for a novella, or 40,000 to 60,000 for a light novel. That's totally manageable in a 12 to 18-hour writing day with structured breaks and a bit of stamina. Remember, your goal is to tell a complete, compelling story—not necessarily the longest one ever written. A lot of bestselling eBooks these days fall in that novella range because readers love fast, bingeable fiction. And ChatGPT makes that possible because it lets you keep moving forward without burning time reinventing the wheel.

The key mindset here is creative flow over perfectionism. This isn't the day to polish every sentence like a poet or obsess over comma placement. This is the day to get the story out, chapter by chapter, paragraph by paragraph, scene by scene. ChatGPT helps you maintain that momentum. You can revise later. You can fix awkward phrasing or add flourishes in the editing stage. But right now, you're riding a creative wave—and the AI is your surfboard.

Let's not forget the energy of excitement. One of the most powerful fuels for creativity is momentum. When you know you're making fast progress and hitting major milestones, you actually feel more energized. There's a kind of addictive joy to watching your story take shape right in front of you, hour by hour. It's the opposite of the grind. You're not trudging through a book for months on end. You're diving in, getting lost in the world, and coming out the other side with something real. Something finished. And let's be honest, finished feels fantastic.

But it's not just about speed—it's about unlocking new ways to write. ChatGPT doesn't take away your creativity, it enhances it. It gives you the power to try ideas you wouldn't normally consider. It lets you test alternate scenes in seconds. You can ask it to rewrite a chapter in a different style or voice. You can request metaphors, punchier dialogue, inner thoughts, action descriptions, or character insights—and it will generate results in seconds. You're still the captain of the ship, but you've got a crew now. And they work fast.

Of course, writing a fiction book in one day does take a bit of preparation. You'll need to schedule a full day, stay hydrated, take short breaks, and keep your distractions to a minimum. It helps to start with a general plan for your story—even if it's just a one-liner or an idea for the final scene. But don't worry, we'll go over all those steps in detail throughout the chapters to come. You'll learn how to manage time, structure your day, keep your story flowing, and even how to rest your eyes without losing your thread.

At the end of the day—literally—you'll have something very few writers manage in a year: a finished book. It might not be perfect. It might need some smoothing or expansion later. But it will be done. And that's something powerful. There's a shift that happens in your mindset when you prove to yourself that it can be done. Suddenly, the whole writing game changes. The blank page doesn't scare you anymore. Writer's block loses its power. And you've got a new tool in your belt—AI-assisted fiction creation that respects your imagination and matches your momentum.

So if you've ever dreamed of writing a novel but felt like you didn't have the time, or the focus, or the tools—this is your moment. Because with ChatGPT at your side, one day is all you need. Let's dive in.

Getting Your Mind in Gear before You Begin

Before you start hammering out words and letting ChatGPT spin story gold with you, you need to do something just as important as plotting or crafting characters—you need to get your mind in the right gear. This might sound like one of those fluffy, motivational pep talks, but trust me, this part matters. Writing a fiction book in a single day isn't just about how fast you can type or how clever your plot is—it's about entering the right mental space to flow, focus, and commit to a long, exhilarating stretch of creativity. If your brain is scattered, distracted, or hesitant, the process becomes a chore. But when your mind is primed and sharp, the entire experience becomes an adventure.

The first shift you need to make is believing that this is possible. Doubt is like sand in the gears—it slows everything down. So let's start by wiping away the idea that great fiction needs months or years to write. That might be true for some writers and some types of books, but it's not the rule. What you're doing here is generating a complete, cohesive, compelling story—not necessarily the next epic in ten volumes. You're creating something that can stand on its own. It might be 20,000 words, or 50,000, or somewhere in between. But the key is: it's a full story, and that's what counts. Start by accepting that you can do it. And not just do it—you can enjoy doing it.

Now it's time to declutter your mental space. Think of your brain as a writing studio. If that studio is filled with noise—emails to answer, notifications pinging, dishes in the sink, errands calling your name—then your focus will constantly be pulled in a dozen directions. To write a book in a day, you need to create what I like to call a "creative vacuum." That's a dedicated bubble of time and attention where the only thing that matters is the story you're about to tell. You can create this by choosing a time when you won't be interrupted, turning off your phone or switching on focus mode, and letting everyone around you know that you're off the grid for the next stretch of hours. Clear your schedule. This is your writing day.

Next up is warming up your creative muscles. If you jump into writing cold, it can take a while to hit your stride. But if you ease in, it all flows faster. You might want to take ten or fifteen minutes before your writing day officially starts to play with ChatGPT on a few light prompts. Ask it to generate some quirky story ideas. Play with genres. Make it write a silly scene with an angry wizard and a talking sandwich—anything that shakes loose the stiffness in your thinking and gets you smiling. You're not trying to write anything serious yet. You're just reminding your brain that it's allowed to play. And play is where great storytelling starts.

Once you're warmed up, the next step is setting your intention. Why are you writing this book today? Maybe it's for fun. Maybe it's an experiment. Maybe it's something you've always wanted to do but never had the time for. Get clear on that. Write it down if it helps. When you know why you're doing this, it anchors you. And when you get tired later or hit a bump in the story, you can come back to that reason and let it refuel you. This whole thing isn't about perfection—it's about expression. You're telling a story that didn't exist yesterday. That's magic.

You should also take a moment to visualize success. Picture the end of your day, when you close your laptop or lean back in your chair and realize you've done it. You wrote a book. That moment is powerful. It doesn't just give you a sense of accomplishment—it changes how you see yourself as a writer. You're not someone who's "trying to write." You're someone who finishes. Someone who creates. That mindset shift begins now, with the simple act of seeing it before it happens.

There's also a practical side to mental preparation, and that's getting familiar with your creative tools. If you're using ChatGPT for the first time, take a few minutes before the writing sprint to get comfortable with how it responds to you. Try giving it different styles of prompts—short and open-ended, long and specific. See how it handles dialogue, action scenes, or emotional beats. You don't need to master anything here. You just want to feel confident navigating the conversation so that when you're in the writing zone, you're not second-guessing how to ask for what you need.

Set your expectations clearly for the writing day ahead. Understand that not every sentence will be perfect, and not every chapter will pour out like melted chocolate. There will be moments when you'll get stuck, lose focus, or question the direction your story's taking. That's totally normal. What matters is that you keep going. If a scene isn't working, ask ChatGPT for a rewrite. If the pacing feels off, ask it to summarize and restructure. If a character's dialogue falls flat, ask for new lines in a different tone. This tool is flexible—it's here to help you pivot fast and stay in flow. But that only works if you commit to staying in the process and not getting hung up on tiny details.

Another thing that helps get your mind in gear is preparing your physical environment to support your focus. This doesn't mean you need a Pinterest-worthy writing nook. Just something that makes you feel comfortable and grounded. That could be a clean desk, a cozy chair, your favorite playlist in the background, or a big cup of coffee or tea. Have snacks and water nearby so you don't have to break your flow when hunger hits. The fewer disruptions you allow in your physical space, the more your mental focus can lock in and stay sharp.

Finally, give yourself permission to be surprised. One of the best parts of using ChatGPT is that it can offer you ideas and plot turns that you never would've come up with on your own. That's not cheating—it's collaboration. You're the director, the visionary, the soul of the story. ChatGPT is the assistant who helps bring it all to life faster than you could alone. So keep your curiosity alive throughout the writing day. If something unexpected pops up in the story and you like it, run with it. If a scene evolves into something deeper or stranger than you planned, explore it. That openness will keep your creative energy buzzing.

So before we dive into building plots, crafting characters, or sculpting dialogue, take a breath. Let the world fall away. Step into the headspace of a writer on a mission. Today, you're not waiting for inspiration—you're generating it. You're not getting ready to write—you're writing. And with the help of ChatGPT, you're about to do something bold, focused, and wildly satisfying. Your mind is clear, your space is set, and your fingers are ready. Let's tell a story.

How to Ask ChatGPT for Original and Unique Story Ideas

Let's get one thing out of the way right now—ChatGPT isn't going to hand you the next literary masterpiece on a silver platter without you putting in a little thought. That's not because it can't generate brilliant story ideas. It can. But the magic happens when *you* learn how to ask the right questions. ChatGPT is like a super-powered creative partner who responds to the way you lead the dance. If you feed it vague, generic prompts, it'll give you vague, generic story ideas. But when you're clear, curious, and intentional, you unlock a level of creativity that's honestly kind of mind-blowing. The trick is learning how to communicate your needs in a way that gets those original and unique sparks flying.

Let's start with what *not* to do. If you ask ChatGPT something like "give me a story idea," it'll most likely give you something pretty basic. Maybe a hero on a quest, or a detective solving a murder, or a love story with a predictable arc. These templates are fine, but they're not going to make your fiction stand out. The problem isn't ChatGPT—it's that you haven't given it anything specific to work with. When your prompt is broad, the output will usually lean toward the familiar. That's just how language models work. They predict based on common patterns, unless you guide them in a new direction.

Now here's where the fun begins. Instead of asking for *a* story, start with a vibe, a weird concept, a mashup of genres, or a strange "what if" question. This is where ChatGPT really shines. Ask it things like, "Give me a story idea about a romance between two rival food critics during an alien invasion," or "What if a time traveler got stuck in a simulation run by their future self?" or even, "Imagine a noir detective story set entirely inside a haunted virtual reality." Suddenly, you're getting ideas that are quirky, layered, and unexpected. The more specific and playful you are, the more ChatGPT can surprise you with something genuinely fresh.

You can also give it a list of ingredients to build from. Tell it, "Give me five story ideas that include a ghost, a submarine, and a forgotten language." Or, "Create a story premise involving a retired hitman, a violin, and a secret beneath a library." You're creating constraints, but those constraints force the AI to get creative. You're pushing it off the beaten path and into the terrain of originality. It's like giving it a handful of Lego pieces and saying, "Make something wild." And it does.

Another powerful way to use ChatGPT is to ask for *variations* on a basic idea. Maybe you've already got the seed of a story, but it feels a little too familiar. Ask ChatGPT to spin it in five different directions. Say something like, "Here's a basic plot: a woman wakes up with no memory and discovers she's being hunted. Give me five variations that add a twist or unexpected genre element." You might get answers like: "She's actually an AI in a synthetic body," or "She's reliving the same day in a parallel dimension," or "Her memory loss is staged to protect her from a mind-controlling parasite." Each one of those spins could be the foundation of a completely unique book.

Don't be afraid to get weird with your requests. Ask for surreal story ideas, absurd premises, or genre-defying hybrids. "Give me a story idea that reads like Kafka and Quentin Tarantino co-wrote a fantasy adventure," or "What if The Great Gatsby took place on Mars?" These kinds of off-the-wall prompts open up creative spaces you may not have explored on your own. The key is to lean into the unexpected. Original stories often come from strange corners, and ChatGPT is happy to take you there if you give it permission.

One trick that works wonders is asking ChatGPT to write you a story *blurb* or *logline* based on a theme or tone you want to explore. Let's say you're interested in writing about redemption, grief, or obsession. Ask it, "Give me five story blurbs that explore the theme of obsession in different genres." You might get a psychological thriller, a sci-fi mystery, a dark romance, a gothic horror, and a legal drama—all dealing with obsession in a different way. You now have five completely different entry points into one emotional theme, and each one could become a powerful, original book.

You can also use comparison prompts. Try something like, "Give me a story idea that feels like Black Mirror crossed with The Handmaid's Tale," or "Imagine a story in the tone of a Studio Ghibli film, but with the plot of a political thriller." This technique lets you triangulate your creative intent. You're giving the AI a tone and a structure, or an aesthetic and a theme. The results can be incredibly inventive. It's like mixing colors on a palette and discovering a new shade.

Another way to dig deeper is to *refine* what ChatGPT gives you. Don't just stop at the first idea it spits out. Ask follow-up questions. "Can you make it darker?" "Can you add a romantic subplot?" "What's a surprising twist for this premise?" "How could this idea work in a different setting?" The real magic often happens in those second and third layers of the conversation. That's where the ideas evolve into something unique to *you*. You're not just generating content—you're shaping it through curiosity and intuition.

And if you want something truly personal, try asking ChatGPT for ideas that reflect your own fears, dreams, or fascinations. "Give me a story idea about someone who's terrified of losing control." Or, "Create a story based on the feeling of being invisible in your own life." When you infuse your prompts with emotional truth, the ideas come back with more weight, more depth. You're not just generating something random—you're mining something real, and ChatGPT is helping you turn that into narrative gold.

At this point, you're probably seeing how powerful the process can be when you take the lead. ChatGPT is like a thousand idea engines all rolled into one. It doesn't get tired, it doesn't run out of inspiration, and it doesn't judge. You can throw wild prompts at it all day long, and it will keep delivering. The challenge isn't whether it can give you original story ideas—it's whether you're willing to explore beyond your usual comfort zone and keep digging until one of those ideas sparks something inside you.

So before you write your book, spend some time having this idea jam session with ChatGPT. Go wide. Go strange. Go deep. Ask for more than you need. Let the bad ideas come too, because sometimes they lead to the great ones. You don't need the *perfect* idea to start—just a compelling one. One that makes you lean forward, grin a little, and say, "Yeah... I want to write *that*." When you feel that spark, you're ready to move forward. And remember, if you ever get stuck along the way, ChatGPT is right there with you, ready to help spin the next idea, the next twist, the next scene. All it takes is the right question.

Finding the Genre That Excites You

Before you start writing your one-day fiction book with ChatGPT, there's one big decision that will shape everything that follows—choosing your genre. This isn't just about filing your book neatly into a category. Genre is the emotional promise you're making to your reader. It's the mood, the energy, the structure, and even the pacing of your story. Picking the right genre does more than just narrow your focus—it plugs you directly into the kind of story that excites you. And excitement is exactly what you need if you're about to commit to an intense day of storytelling.

You don't need to overthink this. The simplest way to start is to ask yourself, "What kind of stories do I love reading or watching?" If you find yourself glued to psychological thrillers, drawn into epic fantasy worlds, or laughing your way through romantic comedies, that's a clue. The genre you naturally enjoy consuming is often the best place to start writing. When you write in a genre you love, your energy stays high, your ideas come quicker, and you don't second-guess your instincts as much. You know what you like, so you can follow that internal compass as you shape your own version of it.

ChatGPT can help you explore your genre preferences, too. If you're unsure what genre excites you most—or if you're torn between a few—you can ask for short summaries of each genre and the kinds of tropes they use. Try something like, "Describe the core elements of a cozy mystery vs. a hard-boiled detective story," or "What are the emotional beats of a coming-of-age drama compared to a dystopian sci-fi?" When you read those breakdowns, you'll feel a tug toward one more than the others. That tug is your signal.

You can also ask ChatGPT to give you sample story ideas across different genres to help you compare. Try a prompt like, "Give me three story premises for each of these genres: horror, romance, sci-fi, and fantasy." As you read through the suggestions, pay attention to what lights you up. Do you feel intrigued, curious, amused, inspired? Do certain ideas make you want to start writing immediately? That's the genre that's pulling you in. And once you know it, the writing becomes a lot easier because you're following genuine excitement instead of trying to force something you think you're "supposed" to write.

There's also room to play with genre combinations if you're feeling adventurous. You might love romance, but also crave suspense. Maybe you're into science fiction, but you want the emotional depth of a family drama. You can absolutely blend genres—just make sure you know which one is leading the dance. If you write a sci-fi romance, for example, ask yourself whether your reader will be more invested in the love story or the futuristic world-building. Having that clarity helps keep the tone and pacing consistent throughout the book, even if you're mixing elements.

When you've picked a genre, ChatGPT can help you understand the typical structure and emotional rhythm that comes with it. Ask for common tropes, character types, conflicts, and resolutions within that genre. Say something like, "What are the most used story beats in a heist thriller?" or "How is tension typically built in a gothic horror?" Knowing these patterns gives you a roadmap you can follow or intentionally break. Either way, you're writing with awareness, which gives your story a stronger backbone.

One of the best reasons to lock in your genre early is because it helps ChatGPT serve you better. If you tell it, "I want to write a cozy mystery set in a small town where the local librarian solves crimes," you'll get better outlines, scene prompts, and dialogue than if you just say, "Help me write a story." The more you narrow the scope, the more specific and helpful the AI's responses become. It becomes a tool tailored to your chosen genre, rather than a general idea generator.

You should also consider how much research or world-building your genre will require—especially since you're aiming to write a book in a single day. Some genres, like historical fiction or high fantasy, demand more setup. That doesn't mean you can't write them in a day, but you'll want to plan accordingly. You can use ChatGPT to do quick research or create a world-building outline ahead of time. Or you can choose a genre that's more grounded in everyday life, like romance, slice-of-life drama, or crime fiction, which typically require less setup and more emotional or plot-driven writing.

It's worth noting that genre also influences pacing. A thriller moves fast, with short, punchy chapters and high tension. A literary drama might breathe more slowly, focusing on introspection and internal conflict. A romantic comedy has a rhythm of build-up, misunderstanding, and emotional payoff. When you choose your genre, you're also choosing the pace at which you'll write, the tone of your language, and the kind of scenes that make up your narrative. It's like selecting a musical tempo—everything else moves in time with it.

If you're still on the fence about what to write, use ChatGPT to help you imagine yourself at the finish line. Ask, "What kind of story would leave me feeling most satisfied when I finish writing it?" Let the AI help you visualize your end goal, and you may discover that what you really want to write isn't what you thought. Sometimes the genre we need to write comes from an emotional place rather than a logical one. Maybe you've had a tough week and need the escape of fantasy. Maybe you've been feeling nostalgic and want to write something heartfelt. Listen to that internal voice—it always knows.

Once you've picked your genre, commit to it for this one-day project. You're not locked in for life. You can write something completely different tomorrow. But for today, having one clear genre focus will keep you from wandering and second-guessing. It's the structure around your creativity, not a cage. And with ChatGPT in your corner, that structure becomes a powerful launchpad for a full book you can start—and finish—before the day is done.

So take a moment. Close your eyes. Picture the kind of story that would be the most fun, the most energizing, the most *you*. That's your genre. Let's get to work.

Starting with the End: Why Backward Thinking Works

One of the smartest moves you can make when writing a fiction book in a single day with ChatGPT is starting with the end. It might seem counterintuitive. After all, we're used to thinking linearly—beginning, middle, end. But when you flip that around and start with the climax or final scene in mind, the entire story becomes easier to plot, more cohesive, and, surprisingly, faster to write. That's the power of backward thinking. It gives you clarity, direction, and a story that feels like it was always meant to happen.

Think about how many writers start a story with only a vague idea and then end up wandering in the middle, unsure of how to get to the conclusion. That's where most books stall. But when you start by imagining your ending—the twist, the triumph, the heartbreak, the final confrontation—you're giving yourself a target to aim for. Suddenly, every scene you write becomes a step toward that end. It all makes sense, because you're building a road to somewhere, not just driving aimlessly hoping to find a story.

ChatGPT thrives on clarity. If you know how your story ends, you can ask the AI to work backward with you. You can say something like, "The story ends with the protagonist walking away from a burning building, believing they've lost everything—but actually they've saved the world. Help me outline the events that logically lead to this moment." ChatGPT will start mapping out the pieces you need—the betrayal, the loss, the discovery, the conflict, the choice. In a few minutes, you've gone from a dramatic final image to a solid story arc.

The end of your story is often where your theme comes into focus. Whether your book is about redemption, justice, love, revenge, or freedom, the resolution shows what the story was really about all along. By deciding the ending first, you lock in that emotional and thematic anchor. You know what kind of transformation your characters need to go through. You know what kind of payoff the reader is waiting for. That means you can shape the rest of the book to build toward that moment, making everything tighter and more emotionally satisfying.

You don't need to know *every* detail of your ending. It doesn't have to be a perfectly polished scene with final lines of dialogue ready to go. It just needs to be a vision. A sense of what happens, where your characters are emotionally, what the world looks like after everything they've been through. Do they win? Lose? Sacrifice something? Discover a truth? Escape? You're choosing the final note—the tone and meaning you want to leave the reader with. Once you have that, the rest is about reverse-engineering how to get there.

Using backward thinking also helps avoid unnecessary subplots and distractions. It keeps your book streamlined, which is crucial when writing in a single day. You're not padding the story with filler because everything you write has to serve the journey toward the end. You can ask ChatGPT for help maintaining that focus. Try, "Based on this ending, what scenes are essential to support this character arc?" or "What moments need to happen to make this ending feel earned?" The AI becomes your brainstorming partner, not just for coming up with ideas, but for testing their narrative logic.

One powerful technique is to actually write the ending first. Type it out—describe the setting, the emotions, the actions, the final twist or revelation. It might only be a few paragraphs or a full final chapter. That piece of writing becomes your anchor. You can keep referring to it as you work through the rest of the story. It's your North Star. If you're using ChatGPT to help generate chapters or scenes, you can paste that ending at the top of your session and say, "We're building toward this—help me write the middle chapters that set this up." The results will be more consistent, more intentional, and more emotionally resonant.

There's something creatively liberating about knowing how it ends. You don't have to second-guess yourself at every turn. You don't have to keep asking, "Where is this going?" Because you already know. That knowledge gives you the freedom to explore within a framework. You can take detours, add depth, or surprise yourself with character decisions—but you always have a clear sense of direction. That's what makes the writing process smoother, and it's especially helpful when you're trying to write a full book in one burst.

Backward thinking also unlocks better twists. If you know what the twist is at the end, you can layer in foreshadowing, misdirection, or emotional build-up that makes it land harder. ChatGPT is especially good at helping you reverse-engineer clues. You can say, "The twist is that the mentor is actually the villain. What subtle signs can I plant earlier to make this believable but not obvious?" And just like that, you've got a breadcrumb trail that guides your reader to the reveal without ruining the surprise.

This technique doesn't just work for plot—it's also powerful for character development. If you know that your protagonist ends the story as a selfless hero, but begins as a selfish loner, then you've defined their arc. You can then ask ChatGPT, "Help me chart the turning points in this character's emotional journey from selfishness to sacrifice." Now you're building a story where the character growth feels natural, because you've already decided where they need to arrive. Their actions, decisions, and relationships all grow out of that final transformation. Starting with the end also gives you emotional motivation. When you're hours into your writing sprint and you start feeling tired, you can reread your ending and remind yourself what you're working toward. That emotional payoff—the triumph, the resolution, the catharsis—is your fuel. It reminds you that this story matters. It reminds you that you're not just generating text, you're crafting something with a heartbeat and a destination.

And when it's all said and done, starting with the end gives you something writers don't always get—closure. You know the full arc. You know what it was all building toward. You don't finish the day feeling unsure if your story went anywhere. You know it landed. You can look at your finished draft and say, "I did that. I made that ending count." That feeling is one of the best rewards in writing. So before you dive into your chapters, outlines, and character descriptions, take a little time to think about how your story ends. Picture it. Write it. Describe it to ChatGPT and build backward from there. This single shift in your process can save you hours of guessing, give your story a clear emotional arc, and make your entire writing day smoother and more satisfying. And the best part? You're in control. You choose how it ends. You choose what matters. And with ChatGPT helping you reverse-engineer it all, that ending is never out of reach.

Crafting a Powerful Climax before Anything Else

The climax of a story is the moment where everything pays off. It's the scene that delivers the emotional or dramatic punch your readers have been waiting for. It's where the character faces their biggest test, where all the rising tension explodes into a choice, an action, or a revelation. So when you're writing a fiction book in one day with ChatGPT, one of the smartest things you can do is build the climax first. Not the opening, not the world-building, not even the dialogue. The climax. That final, intense moment is the heartbeat of your story—and once you've crafted it, everything else becomes a matter of leading the reader there.

Let's start by thinking about what a climax really is. It's not just the biggest explosion or loudest argument. It's the moment of highest emotional and narrative intensity. It's where your character finally faces the consequences of everything they've done, said, or believed. If your story is about redemption, this is where the character has to sacrifice something. If it's about love, this is where they confess, choose, or walk away. If it's a thriller, this is where the truth is exposed and the threat is confronted. This is the moment where the story answers its biggest question.

To build a powerful climax before anything else, you first need to decide what that question is. Ask yourself: what's the emotional or moral dilemma at the center of this story? What's the big thing the protagonist needs to face? Once you know that, you can start to visualize the climax as the ultimate resolution of that question. If the story asks, "Can a person change their nature?" then the climax needs to show the protagonist making a choice that proves they have—or haven't—changed. That clarity anchors the entire book.

ChatGPT can help you create and refine this climax quickly. You can start with a simple prompt like, "My story is about a young hacker trying to escape a corrupt tech empire. What could the climax of this story be?" You'll get ideas that revolve around high-stakes confrontations, big moral decisions, or moments of unexpected vulnerability. From there, you can refine further. "Make it more emotional." "Add a betrayal from a close ally." "What if the villain wins, but it feels like a bittersweet victory for the hero?" Each iteration brings you closer to a climax that feels powerful, specific, and true to your story's tone.

Once you've locked in the basic structure of the climax, get detailed. Write the scene out, even if it's just a rough version. Use ChatGPT to help you flesh out the setting, the mood, the dialogue, and the emotional beats. Ask, "Help me write a scene where the protagonist confronts their father, who has secretly been orchestrating everything behind the scenes." Or, "Describe the moment the main character realizes they were the villain all along." The more vivid the climax becomes in your mind, the more easily you'll shape everything that comes before it.

Writing the climax first also allows you to reverse-engineer the rest of the story. Once you know what happens at the end, you can trace back what needs to happen to make that ending feel earned. What earlier moments set up this final showdown? What lies or secrets need to be revealed along the way? What relationships need to break or deepen? ChatGPT can help here too. Try asking, "What are five key scenes that would logically lead to this climax?" or "What emotional arc does the protagonist need to go through to make this climax believable?" These kinds of questions build a bridge between the beginning and the ending—and that bridge is your story.

Another benefit of starting with the climax is that it helps you avoid wandering in the middle of your book. The infamous "mushy middle" of a novel is where pacing slows and tension drops because the writer isn't sure where they're headed. But when your climax is already written, you're not wandering—you're aiming. Every scene, every chapter is moving in a straight line toward that moment. And if you start to drift, you just look at your climax and recalibrate. It's a built-in compass that keeps you on course.

You can also use the climax to shape your protagonist's arc. If the climax demands bravery, then your protagonist needs to begin the story in fear. If it's about truth, they need to begin in denial. This gives you a clear emotional trajectory for the character, which makes your story more satisfying. Readers love growth. They want to see a character face something hard and come out changed. The climax is proof of that transformation—and writing it first gives you the clearest picture of what that transformation looks like.

Here's another trick. Once you've got your climax written, imagine what happens five minutes after it ends. That little epilogue scene can tell you a lot about the emotional resolution of your story. Are the characters together or apart? Is the world better or worse? Is there a lingering question or a sense of closure? Writing this short moment after the climax helps clarify what tone you're aiming for—triumphant, tragic, hopeful, ironic—and that tone can influence the flavor of the entire book. Ask ChatGPT, "What happens five minutes after the climax?" and see what direction it takes you.

You might also discover that your climax inspires ideas for foreshadowing or symbolism. If your climax involves a confrontation on a rooftop, maybe early in the story you hint at your character's fear of heights. If the final moment hinges on a broken watch or a piece of music, you can seed those elements earlier to create resonance. ChatGPT is great at helping you plant those seeds. Just ask, "What are some objects, images, or themes I could introduce early that would tie into this climax?" and you'll get suggestions that make your story feel tight and intentional.

What makes all of this especially powerful for one-day writing is that it reduces decision fatigue. When you start writing without a clear idea of where you're going, you burn a lot of energy just making choices—what happens next, how characters react, what the stakes are. But when your climax is already in place, those choices become easier. They're not arbitrary. They're guided by the ending you're working toward. That saves time, boosts momentum, and helps you stay in the creative flow for longer stretches. So if you're sitting down to write your book in a day and wondering where to begin, forget the first line. Forget the backstory. Start with the moment it all explodes, twists, resolves, or transforms. Build the climax. Write it out. Make it pulse with tension, meaning, and consequence. Then, let that moment guide everything else you write. Let it give shape to your plot, depth to your characters, and momentum to your pacing. With that one decision, you've already done half the storytelling work. The rest is just walking the road to get there. And with ChatGPT helping you every step of the way, that road is about to be a lot easier—and a lot more fun—to travel.

Building Your Story Backwards to the Beginning

Once you've got your climax in place—the explosive final moment where everything comes together—it's time to reverse-engineer the entire story from that point. Writing backwards isn't about being quirky or clever. It's a practical, powerful method that makes sure every scene serves a purpose. When you know where you're headed, you don't waste time wandering. You build toward the ending with intention, clarity, and direction. This is especially useful when you're writing a full fiction book in one day using ChatGPT, because it keeps the process smooth, efficient, and creatively energized.

Start by looking at your climax and asking one question: how did the character get here? Not just physically—emotionally, mentally, and circumstantially. What had to happen to make this moment possible? Who did they lose? What truth did they learn? What lie did they believe for too long? The climax of a story is never random. It's a chain reaction set in motion by dozens of smaller moments. Your job now is to work backwards through that chain and figure out what each of those moments looks like. And ChatGPT is here to help you do that in minutes instead of hours.

Let's say your climax is a standoff between two old friends turned enemies. One has a gun. The other has a secret. It's tense, dramatic, and deeply personal. To write the rest of the book, you ask yourself: how did they go from friends to this? What broke their trust? What made them choose opposing sides? You can ask ChatGPT, "What are five events that could lead two best friends to become enemies in a story that ends in a final confrontation?" From there, the model might give you betrayal, ideological conflict, family secrets, romantic entanglements, or moments of failure. These become your key scenes in reverse.

Once you know those key beats, start arranging them in reverse order. The betrayal comes right before the confrontation. The misunderstanding that led to the betrayal comes before that. The moment of temptation, the lie, the deal with the enemy—it all stacks neatly into place. And by the time you reach the beginning of the story, you've laid out a roadmap of how things escalate. It's like seeing a house fully built, then taking it apart piece by piece so you understand how to construct it again from the foundation.

As you move backward through the story, think about the emotional arc of your protagonist. What kind of person are they at the end, and how different are they from who they were at the start? If they've learned something big, then your story becomes about how they learned it. If they've lost everything, then the story is about what they had and how they lost it. ChatGPT can help you shape that journey by asking questions like, "If my protagonist ends the story sacrificing themselves for others, what earlier scenes could show their selfish nature?" That contrast makes the arc feel real and earned.

This backward-building method also helps with pacing. One common mistake writers make—especially when racing to write a book in one day—is starting too slow or wandering off course in the middle. But when you write backward, every chapter is chosen because it's necessary. There's no filler. Every scene serves the next one. ChatGPT can help you summarize each chapter's purpose as you build backward: "What would need to happen right before this scene for it to make sense?" It's like snapping puzzle pieces into place until you've completed the full picture.

Another advantage to this method is that it allows for better layering. You can plant foreshadowing more naturally when you already know what it's leading to. If the final act includes a surprise reveal, you can now place hints earlier in the story that the reader will subconsciously pick up on. Ask ChatGPT, "What are three subtle ways to hint that the mentor is actually the villain?" or "How can I set up a twist where the protagonist is unknowingly being watched?" These moments become more organic because you're writing them with the end already burned into your creative brain.

As you work backward, don't worry about writing everything in perfect order. Think in terms of scenes or turning points. You can write chapter 15 before chapter 4 if that's what's flowing. Let ChatGPT help you fill in the gaps as you go. Say, "Based on this plot so far, what would be a logical scene to come before this?" and let it offer suggestions. The writing process becomes more fluid, more exploratory, and way more fun. You're constantly sculpting, shaping, and connecting instead of building blindly.

You'll also notice that when you write backwards, characters become more consistent. Since you already know how they end up—brave, broken, redeemed, transformed—you can write earlier scenes that reflect the opposite. If your character ends up forgiving someone, then earlier scenes can show how deep the resentment ran. If they end up alone, then the story becomes a journey through lost connections. ChatGPT can help map out those emotional beats by asking, "What scenes could show the erosion of a friendship over time?" or "What events might cause someone to fear intimacy?" These deeper layers make your book feel more authentic and emotionally rich, even if you wrote it in one day.

Once you've reverse-mapped all the major turning points—from the climax to the midpoint to the inciting incident—you'll eventually land at your beginning. And here's the beautiful thing: it won't feel like a beginning at all. It will feel like the natural starting point of a journey that has purpose and momentum. You won't be staring at a blank page wondering how to start. You'll already know what needs to happen. You'll know who the character is, what they're missing, and what they're about to face. That makes writing the first few chapters incredibly satisfying instead of stressful.

When you're done building backward, you can ask ChatGPT to help you re-sequence everything in forward order. Just say, "Help me organize these story beats into a standard three-act structure starting from the beginning." You'll get a clean, logical progression that you can then flesh out scene by scene. The cool part is, since the climax is already written, and the major turning points are laid out, the rest of the writing moves quickly. You're no longer searching for the story. You're simply filling in the details.

So if you've ever struggled with where to start, or found yourself drowning in the middle of your book, try going in reverse. Build your story from the climax back to the inciting incident. Ask questions, get specific, and let ChatGPT walk with you every step of the way. What you'll find is that when you write backward, you end up with a story that feels complete, purposeful, and emotionally satisfying. And most importantly—it gets written. That's the whole goal here. A finished book. A full arc. A complete experience. And it all starts with looking at the end and saying, "Now how did we get here?"

Creating a Plot That Pulls Readers Forward

When you're writing a fiction book in one day with ChatGPT, you don't have time for slow starts, meandering subplots, or chapters that wander off course. What you need is a plot that grabs your reader from the beginning and keeps them turning pages without ever feeling like they can stop. A plot that pulls readers forward is more than just a sequence of events—it's a rhythm, a pulse, a sense that something bigger is coming and they just have to see what it is. That kind of momentum makes your story exciting to read and energizing to write, especially when you're racing the clock to finish in a single day.

So how do you create that kind of plot? You start by thinking in terms of movement. A strong plot is never static. Something is always changing. Characters are growing, relationships are shifting, secrets are unraveling, and tensions are building. You can think of your plot like a chain reaction: each event triggers the next. Every chapter causes something else to happen, raising the stakes, deepening the conflict, or twisting the reader's expectations. If your story ever stops moving forward, it risks losing the reader—and losing your writing momentum. That's why pace and propulsion are your best friends.

One of the best ways to create this sense of constant movement is by setting up story questions early on. These aren't just small mysteries or puzzles. These are the burning questions that drive the reader's curiosity. What's really going on? Who can be trusted? Will they survive? Can the relationship be saved? ChatGPT can help you frame these questions right from the start. You can ask, "What are some story-driving questions for a mystery about a woman who wakes up in a town that doesn't exist on any map?" The answers you get become the engines of your story, giving each scene a reason to exist and a direction to go.

To keep readers hooked, every chapter should end with something unresolved. It doesn't have to be a massive cliffhanger every time, but there should always be a reason for the reader to keep going. A discovery, a shift in tone, a new piece of information, a character making a surprising decision—these are all little pulses of forward motion. ChatGPT can help you brainstorm chapter endings by asking, "What's a compelling way to end this scene so readers want to keep going?" It will generate options that hint at danger, mystery, or emotional stakes, all of which keep the reader engaged.

Another important element in a forward-pulling plot is escalation. You don't want your story to stay flat or repetitive. Each scene should increase the pressure. The obstacles get harder. The emotions get heavier. The risks get bigger. ChatGPT can help you structure this escalation by asking, "What are five escalating challenges my protagonist could face on their way to the climax?" When you layer those into your outline, you're building a story that grows in intensity, and that growth keeps the momentum alive.

But it's not just about what happens. It's about *why* it happens. A plot that moves forward with purpose is always tied to character motivation. If the protagonist doesn't want anything, or isn't driven to act, then the story just sort of floats along. But if your main character wants something badly—love, revenge, freedom, truth—then every plot beat becomes a step toward or away from that goal. You can ask ChatGPT, "What is a compelling motivation for a protagonist in a sci-fi survival story?" and use the answer to drive every major plot decision. When motivation is strong and clear, plot momentum naturally follows.

Conflict is the fuel that powers your story's engine. Whether it's external (a killer on the loose, a system that oppresses, a secret that threatens to be exposed) or internal (guilt, fear, shame, a difficult choice), conflict adds tension to every scene. You can use ChatGPT to layer both types of conflict into your plot. Ask, "What's a good internal conflict to mirror this external struggle?" or "How can I raise the stakes in this scene without adding more action?" You'll get ideas that add depth and complexity to the plot without dragging it down.

Another trick for building momentum is to use the cause-and-effect rule. Each chapter should be connected to the one before it not by coincidence, but by consequence. This happened, so now this happens. A choice leads to a result, which creates a new challenge, which leads to a new choice. ChatGPT can help you plot using this logic by asking, "If the protagonist just escaped the villain's trap, what's a natural consequence of that action that sets up the next scene?" You're no longer just inventing random plot points—you're building a chain of logic that pulls the story forward.

Timing matters too. If you spend too long in the setup phase, your story might lose its spark before it catches fire. So get into the action fast. Start with movement, mystery, or emotion. Let readers feel like they've been dropped into something already happening. Then, gradually reveal what's going on as the characters react and adapt. If you're not sure how to start strong, just tell ChatGPT, "Write the opening paragraph of a thriller that starts with the main character on the run." You'll get a draft that launches the story immediately, and you can revise it to match your tone and style.

You can also keep the momentum high by adding small, periodic twists. Not the giant, end-of-story kind, but little surprises that keep readers on their toes. A hidden message, a betrayal, a sudden change in a character's behavior—these keep the story from feeling predictable. ChatGPT is a great source for mini-twists. Just ask, "What's a subtle twist I can add halfway through a romantic comedy?" and let the ideas flow. You can sprinkle these throughout the plot to create moments of surprise and spark.

When you build a plot that pulls readers forward, you also make your job as the writer a lot easier. You don't get stuck wondering what to write next, because every scene has a reason to exist and a direction to move in. You don't lose energy halfway through, because you're constantly building toward something. And with ChatGPT in your corner, you can keep the ideas flowing all day long. If you lose steam or feel stuck, just describe what's happening in the story so far and ask, "What would be a great next scene that keeps things moving?" The AI will give you options, and one of them is almost guaranteed to get you excited again.

So before you dive into writing your full draft, take the time to build a plot that pulls. Focus on momentum, cause and effect, character motivation, escalating tension, and unresolved questions. Ask ChatGPT for help with each of those elements, shaping a story that moves like a current—pulling the reader through it, and pulling you as the writer through the process of finishing the book. When your plot has pull, writing becomes a ride. And in a one-day challenge like this, that's exactly the kind of energy you need.

Outlining a Whole Novel in Under an Hour

If the idea of outlining a whole novel in under an hour sounds impossible, especially when you're about to write it in a single day, then it's time to change the way you look at outlining. You don't need a color-coded spreadsheet, ten pages of character dossiers, or scene cards stuck to a wall with string. What you need is clarity, purpose, and speed—and thankfully, ChatGPT is built to handle exactly that. With the right approach, you can generate a complete, compelling novel outline that gives you a roadmap to follow from beginning to end, all within an hour or even less.

The biggest misconception about outlining is that it has to be rigid or exhaustive. It doesn't. A good outline doesn't strangle your creativity; it gives it direction. It's a plan you can follow, shift, or rework as you write, but it always helps you keep moving forward. And when you're aiming to write your entire book today, that movement is everything. Outlining fast is all about trusting the structure, tapping into your instinct for story, and letting ChatGPT handle the heavy lifting on the structural side while you steer the creative vision.

Start with a strong premise. This is your one-sentence summary of the story, also known as a logline or hook. It should include your protagonist, their goal, what stands in their way, and the stakes if they fail. If you're struggling to come up with a logline, ask ChatGPT for help: "Give me five logline ideas for a thriller about a woman who finds a mysterious device in her attic." Once you land on one that feels exciting, that's your foundation. Everything else will branch off from that.

With your premise in hand, move to the big three: beginning, middle, and end. These don't need to be detailed—just a short paragraph each. The beginning introduces the character, their world, and the initial problem. The middle raises the stakes and deepens the conflict. The end is the climax and resolution. You can give ChatGPT your premise and ask, "Outline a beginning, middle, and end for this story." It'll generate a rough skeleton that gives you a sense of direction and progression. You can tweak it or ask for alternatives until it feels right.

From there, break the story into ten to fifteen chapters. Don't worry about getting them perfect. You're just mapping the beats—the turning points, major scenes, or emotional shifts that keep the story moving. Ask ChatGPT, "Based on this outline, break this into 12 chapter summaries, each one building on the last." What you'll get is a chapter-by-chapter breakdown that gives you a basic goal for each part of the story. Some chapters will focus on action, others on character decisions or emotional growth. You'll start to see a rhythm, and that rhythm is what will guide you when it's time to write fast.

Don't forget your character arcs. While you're mapping the plot, also think about how your main character changes from beginning to end. Does your protagonist start out afraid and end up courageous? Do they begin selfish and become selfless? ChatGPT can help you reverse-engineer this arc. Just say, "What are five turning points in a character's journey from cowardice to bravery?" Those turning points can then become moments you highlight in your outline, giving the emotional side of your story as much structure as the plot.

You can also add a quick outline of your supporting characters. Just a sentence or two each to define their role, relationship to the protagonist, and how they influence the plot. Ask ChatGPT, "Who are three interesting side characters that could support this story and provide conflict or emotional weight?" You'll get ideas for mentors, foils, love interests, or antagonists who can enrich the world and give your protagonist something to react to, support, or struggle against.

If your story involves a mystery, a twist, or a secret that gets revealed later, make sure you map that out in the outline too. Ask ChatGPT, "What are some clever ways to reveal a secret over the course of a 12-chapter story?" Then plug those beats into your outline so the reveal builds naturally and doesn't feel forced. You'll be surprised how easily you can control tension and surprise just by planning where to drop specific pieces of information.

Once your outline starts to take shape, check for cause and effect. Each chapter or scene should lead into the next. Something happens, which causes something else to happen. You want a chain of events, not just a list of scenes. Ask ChatGPT to review your outline and point out where the logic might be weak or where motivation is missing. This step only takes a few minutes but can make a big difference in how cohesive your final draft feels.

You can also build optional prompts into your outline. Under each chapter heading, write a note to yourself like, "Explore tension between protagonist and mentor here," or "Introduce the hidden clue in a subtle way." These guideposts will help you stay on track when you're writing fast. If you want, ChatGPT can generate these notes for you. Just say, "Give me writing prompts for each of these chapters to deepen character and tension."

By the time you've done all of this—which really can happen in less than an hour—you'll have a working outline that includes your premise, beginning-middle-end overview, chapter-by-chapter structure, character arcs, emotional beats, and maybe even a few notes on theme or tone. It doesn't need to be perfect. It just needs to be enough. Enough to keep you moving. Enough to remove the guesswork. Enough to give you confidence that this story has shape, purpose, and a satisfying arc.

And remember, the outline isn't set in stone. As you write, you'll discover new ideas. You'll hear a better line of dialogue. You'll change your mind about a twist. That's fine. Let the story evolve if it needs to. The outline is your safety net. It's what keeps you from falling into the black hole of "what happens next?" And with ChatGPT, that net is fast, flexible, and built to evolve with you.

So if you're staring at the blank screen wondering how to begin, don't dive into chapter one right away. Take the time—just one hour or less—to map the shape of your story. Let ChatGPT help you build that structure, from the climax backward to the beginning, one chapter at a time. Then, when you're ready, you'll hit the page running, with a full story already alive in your mind. No hesitation. No confusion. Just pure, focused storytelling, all laid out in front of you, ready to come alive.

Using ChatGPT to Flesh out a Three-Act Structure

The three-act structure is the classic backbone of storytelling. It's not a rigid formula, but more of a reliable rhythm that keeps your story moving with purpose. Act One sets the stage, Act Two builds the tension, and Act Three delivers the payoff. Whether you're writing a romantic comedy, a dystopian thriller, a cozy mystery, or a fantasy epic, the three-act structure is your best friend—especially when you're trying to write an entire book in one day. And guess what? ChatGPT is the perfect tool to help you map that structure out quickly, thoroughly, and in a way that feels completely your own.

You don't need to be a story theorist or a screenwriting guru to use this model. You just need to understand the basic beats and use ChatGPT to generate content that fits into each one. The beauty of this approach is that you can do it in real time, asking for ideas, summaries, or scene outlines on the fly. This saves you the hours you'd normally spend trying to figure out what's supposed to happen next, because ChatGPT can keep you moving by providing suggestions that make structural sense.

Let's start with Act One. This is your setup. It's where you introduce the main character, their world, and the central problem. The most important beat here is the inciting incident—the moment something changes and sets the story in motion. You can ask ChatGPT to help you brainstorm several options: "What are five inciting incidents for a story about a woman who discovers a hidden room in her basement?" From there, you can pick the one that creates the most tension or curiosity and build the early chapters around that event.

In Act One, you also want to establish what the protagonist wants and what's standing in their way. That's the foundation of plot momentum. If you're not sure how to frame this clearly, you can say to ChatGPT, "Help me describe the protagonist's initial goal and what obstacles they face before the midpoint." What you'll get is a strong sense of conflict that drives the story forward into Act Two.

Act Two is the heart of the book. It's where things get messy. Your protagonist is in motion, trying to solve a problem, find something, or reach a goal, but complications arise. This act is usually the longest and most challenging to write because it's easy to lose focus. But with ChatGPT, you can break it down into manageable chunks. Ask, "What are five escalating events that could happen in Act Two of a story about a detective uncovering a conspiracy?" You'll get a list of ideas that build naturally, each one adding tension or forcing the character to grow.

You can also use ChatGPT to help identify the midpoint twist. This is a major event that changes the game—it can be a revelation, a betrayal, a death, a moment of doubt, or a temporary victory. Just say, "What could be a powerful midpoint twist in a sci-fi story where a colony on Mars discovers alien life?" The AI will offer several surprising ideas, one of which might become the emotional or narrative anchor for the second half of your book.

As Act Two progresses, the stakes should rise. The character should face internal and external challenges. You can build this tension using prompts like, "Give me three emotional turning points in Act Two that push the protagonist to their limits," or "What secondary character could be introduced in Act Two to complicate the hero's journey?" You're not just filling space—you're sculpting a story that feels alive and layered.

Act Three is where everything comes to a head. This is your climax and resolution—the confrontation, the decision, the transformation. Since you've already crafted your climax in earlier chapters, you're now building the final chapters to land that moment with impact. Use ChatGPT to help you pace it: "What scenes should happen between the final betrayal and the last battle?" or "How can I build emotional tension leading up to the protagonist's final choice?" These questions help you fine-tune the shape of your ending.

After the climax comes the resolution—the part that often gets rushed or overlooked. Don't skip this. You want to show how the world has changed, how the characters have grown, and what's been lost or gained. Ask ChatGPT, "What are some quiet, meaningful resolution scenes that can follow a dramatic ending?" It might suggest the protagonist returning home, having a final conversation, or simply walking away changed. These small moments make your story linger in the reader's mind.

Throughout the outlining and writing process, you can use the three-act structure like scaffolding. At any point, you can say to ChatGPT, "Remind me where I am in the three-act structure based on these scenes," or "What should happen next in Act Two to keep the pace moving?" It will help you course-correct in real time, so you don't waste energy trying to figure it out on your own. That's the power of having an intelligent writing partner that always has your story structure in mind.

And here's the best part. You can customize the structure to your style. Some stories might be tighter, with just a few big beats in each act. Others might be more expansive, with multiple threads woven together. ChatGPT can handle both. If you're writing a short novella, ask for a condensed version of the three-act structure. If you're writing something longer and more complex, ask for subplots and interwoven character arcs. Just say, "Give me a three-act outline with two subplots that tie into the main story," and watch how quickly it comes together.

Using ChatGPT to flesh out your three-act structure turns what used to be a long and often frustrating process into something fast, fun, and creative. You're not alone with a blank page—you're collaborating with a tool that understands narrative form and can offer new ideas whenever you need them. By leaning into that structure and letting ChatGPT fill in the details, you create a novel framework that's solid, satisfying, and ready to write—today.

So if you're ready to stop guessing and start writing with confidence, embrace the three-act structure. Let ChatGPT help you shape each act, identify the turning points, and map out the emotional flow. Once it's all laid out, you won't just feel like you can write this novel in a day—you'll feel excited to do it. Because now, you're not just writing. You're storytelling with intention, and that changes everything.

Developing a Believable and Memorable Protagonist

A great story begins and ends with its protagonist. If the reader doesn't care about who the story is happening to, then it doesn't matter how clever the plot is or how exciting the world may be. That's why, when you're writing a fiction book in a single day using ChatGPT, one of the first and most important things you need to do is develop a protagonist that feels real, layered, and unforgettable. You're aiming for someone who can carry the weight of the entire story, someone the reader can root for, worry about, maybe even yell at—but definitely not forget.

The good news is, ChatGPT can help you build that character in record time. With the right questions and direction, you can go from a vague idea to a fully fleshed-out lead character in less than an hour. And once you've got that protagonist in place, the rest of your story has a strong center to orbit around. Every scene, every decision, and every emotional beat becomes easier to write when you understand who this person is and what makes them tick.

Start with the basics. What do they want, and what are they afraid of? These two questions are the heartbeat of any character. The want is the external goal—the thing they're chasing throughout the story. The fear is the internal barrier—the thing that's keeping them from getting what they want or even admitting they want it at all. You can ask ChatGPT something simple like, "Help me create a protagonist who wants justice but is afraid of confronting their past." That's already a compelling contradiction. Now you've got tension, complexity, and room for growth.

It's often helpful to pick a trait or flaw that will cause problems throughout the story. This is where your character gets challenged. Maybe they're too trusting. Maybe they're obsessed with control. Maybe they push people away to avoid getting hurt. Whatever it is, it should affect how they interact with others and how they handle conflict. Ask ChatGPT, "What are some flaws for a character who is a brilliant but emotionally closed-off scientist?" The model will offer flaws that can drive interpersonal tension, make your character more relatable, and give you material for emotional arcs.

Another thing to consider is backstory. You don't need to write five pages of childhood memories, but you do need to know what experiences shaped this person. Why are they the way they are? What wounds haven't healed? What belief do they hold about the world that's going to be tested in your story? You can prompt ChatGPT with something like, "Create a brief backstory for a protagonist who's a former soldier now living off the grid," and get a summary you can plug directly into your outline to guide dialogue, reactions, and choices.

You should also think about voice. How does your protagonist speak and think? Are they sarcastic, poetic, blunt, or overly formal? Voice isn't just about dialogue—it's about the filter through which your reader experiences the story. If you're writing in first person or deep third person, the protagonist's voice will shape the tone of the entire book. ChatGPT can help you with this by generating sample internal monologues. Try something like, "Write a paragraph of internal thoughts from a protagonist who's bitter and funny but secretly hopeful," and see how it captures tone, rhythm, and emotional subtext.

One of the best ways to make your protagonist believable is to ground them in contradictions. Real people are rarely consistent. We say one thing and do another. We want love but sabotage our relationships. We crave freedom but fear change. Ask ChatGPT, "What are some character contradictions that make a protagonist more human?" and you'll get ideas like a cop who hates authority, a romantic who fears commitment, or a loner who desperately wants connection. These contradictions give your character depth and make them feel like someone who lives beyond the page.

Relationships are another layer that can reveal who your protagonist really is. How they interact with others—friends, enemies, love interests, mentors—shows what kind of person they are better than any description can. Ask ChatGPT to help with these dynamics: "Give me a relationship arc between my protagonist and their estranged sibling," or "Describe a mentor-student relationship where both have something to hide." These interactions give your character mirrors, obstacles, and emotional stakes that deepen the story.

The protagonist's journey isn't just about what they do. It's about who they become. You want to show transformation—starting in one emotional or moral place and ending in another. This is what makes a story feel satisfying. It's not just events happening; it's people changing. If you've already written your climax or know how the story ends, you can work backward. Ask ChatGPT, "If my protagonist ends the story sacrificing their happiness for the greater good, how can I show their selfishness earlier in the book?" You'll get key beats to include that make the final transformation feel earned.

Physical details help too, but they're secondary to emotional and psychological layers. Still, a memorable visual can help lock the character in the reader's mind. A scar, a piece of jewelry, a nervous tic, a style of dress—something that makes them pop. You can use prompts like, "What's a distinctive physical trait that could symbolize a character's guilt or grief?" and ChatGPT will offer options that are both symbolic and concrete, helping your protagonist stand out visually.

If you're still unsure about your character's uniqueness, ask ChatGPT to compare them. "What makes this protagonist different from typical action heroes?" or "How could I give a fresh spin to a love-struck underdog character?" These kinds of questions push the character into more original territory, ensuring you're not just writing a copy of someone else's lead from another book or movie.

Once you've gathered all these pieces—desire, fear, flaw, voice, contradiction, backstory, relationships, and arc—you can put them into a short profile. You don't need to overdo it. Just a paragraph or two that summarizes who they are, what drives them, and how they'll change. This profile becomes your guide as you write. Whenever you feel stuck in a scene, you can ask, "What would this character realistically do in this situation?" or "How would their flaw affect this moment?" and ChatGPT will help you stay true to the character's core.

The best protagonists are the ones who linger. They don't have to be perfect. They just have to feel real. They can be broken, funny, annoying, noble, scared, selfish, lost—but they must be human. That's what hooks the reader. That's what gives your story heart. And with ChatGPT, you don't have to spend days or weeks crafting that character. You just have to ask the right questions, follow the threads, and trust your instincts. In a matter of minutes, you'll go from a vague idea to someone you can't wait to spend the day writing about.

And when you finish your book, it won't be the twist, the world, or even the plot that readers remember most—it'll be your protagonist. The one they rooted for, grew with, and didn't want to say goodbye to. That's the power of crafting a believable and memorable lead. And with the help of ChatGPT, it's a power you can tap into right now.

Writing an Antagonist Readers Will Love to Hate

A great story is only as good as its antagonist. Sure, the protagonist is the emotional core—the character we root for—but without a strong antagonist, there's no tension, no stakes, no reason to cheer when the hero wins. The best antagonists do more than cause trouble. They challenge the protagonist, reveal hidden truths, push the story into motion, and force the main character to grow. And when you're writing a fiction book in one day with ChatGPT, crafting a compelling, layered, and loathsome antagonist quickly is totally doable—as long as you ask the right questions and dig a little deeper than just "the bad guy."

First things first: a memorable antagonist isn't evil just for the sake of it. They have a purpose. They have reasons—twisted, maybe, but understandable. That's what makes them believable. And that believability is what makes readers hate them, because they can *almost* understand their motives. Think of the villains who stick with you long after the story ends. They weren't cartoonishly bad. They were smart, charismatic, maybe even sympathetic—until they crossed the line. Your goal isn't to create a one-note villain but a fully developed person whose values, if turned just a few degrees, might resemble your protagonist's.

Start by defining their goal. What do they want, and why do they want it? You can ask ChatGPT, "Help me create an antagonist who believes they're saving the world, even if it means causing mass destruction." That kind of antagonist doesn't see themselves as evil. They think they're doing the hard thing that no one else will. And that self-righteousness is fuel for conflict, because it creates a moral mirror to your protagonist. The reader might hate what they're doing, but they'll understand why they're doing it.

Next, consider their relationship to the protagonist. The closer they are—emotionally, ideologically, or personally—the stronger the tension. An antagonist who used to be a best friend or a mentor hits harder than a stranger. One who believes in the same goal but uses opposite methods creates philosophical conflict. Ask ChatGPT, "Give me antagonist concepts where they share a history with the protagonist," and it'll offer ideas that immediately add emotional weight to your story. Readers love to hate villains who were once loved—or at least trusted.

Flaws and contradictions make antagonists feel human. Maybe your villain preaches order but can't control their own rage. Maybe they're ruthless toward enemies but secretly caring toward one person. Ask ChatGPT, "What are some character flaws that could create tension in an antagonist who's trying to build a utopia?" You'll get nuanced traits that create inner conflict and complexity, which means they won't feel like they're just there to be an obstacle. They'll feel like someone who could almost be the protagonist—if only they made different choices.

Another technique to deepen your antagonist is to give them moments of vulnerability. Not to make them likable, but to make them real. A villain who bleeds, who regrets, who doubts, even if only for a moment, becomes unforgettable. ChatGPT can help you sketch these moments. Try, "Write a scene where the antagonist privately questions their own actions but chooses to move forward anyway." These glimpses behind the mask show readers that this isn't just a monster—it's a person who made a series of choices that led them to darkness.

You can also use ChatGPT to generate scenes from the antagonist's perspective. This is especially useful if your story is written in third person. Ask for an internal monologue, a flashback, or even a conversation between the antagonist and their second-in-command. You might say, "Write a scene where the antagonist explains why they're willing to sacrifice lives for their plan." You'll see the world through their eyes, which helps you write them with more nuance and consistency, even if the reader never sees their POV.

Language matters too. An antagonist's voice—how they speak, how they justify things, what they mock or dismiss—adds texture to the story. You can ask ChatGPT, "Give me some examples of dialogue from a cold, manipulative antagonist who enjoys psychological games," and it will generate lines that you can use or adapt for your scenes. These little touches—the calm confidence, the carefully chosen words, the mocking smile—are what make a villain stand out.

And let's not forget charisma. Many of the best villains are the ones you can't help but watch. They're magnetic, even when they're awful. They have presence. You can ask ChatGPT, "What traits make an antagonist charismatic despite their evil actions?" and you'll get things like intelligence, charm, confidence, or even dark humor. These traits create tension, because the reader might *almost* agree with them—or at least enjoy their scenes, even while rooting for their downfall.

As you build your antagonist, keep tying them back to your protagonist. Their purpose in the story is to challenge the hero. They should represent the opposite path the protagonist *could* take. If your protagonist is learning to open their heart, the antagonist is someone who closed theirs long ago. If the protagonist is seeking justice, the antagonist seeks revenge. This mirror dynamic makes both characters stronger, and it makes the final showdown mean something. You're not just watching two people fight—you're watching two worldviews collide.

It also helps to define the antagonist's arc. Just like your protagonist grows, your antagonist should change—or at least reveal different shades of themselves. Maybe they become more brutal as the story progresses. Maybe they lose control of their plan. Maybe they were being used all along. Ask ChatGPT, "What's a satisfying character arc for a villain who believes they're doing good?" and let it help you shape a journey that feels like more than just a descent into madness.

And don't forget the ending. A great antagonist doesn't just vanish in a puff of smoke. Their downfall should feel earned, emotional, maybe even tragic. Whether they're defeated, imprisoned, redeemed, or destroyed by their own choices, their exit should echo throughout the story. You can ask ChatGPT, "What are some powerful endings for a villain who was once a hero?" and use those suggestions to craft a finale that hits hard.

When you finish writing your antagonist, go back and look at how they're threaded through the story. Are they active, present, and influential? Are they shaping the protagonist's journey, not just popping up when it's convenient? Are their motivations clear and consistent? If not, you can use ChatGPT to help reinforce their presence, suggest scenes, or add tension to moments where they're offscreen but still casting a shadow.

In the end, writing an antagonist readers will love to hate is about depth, intent, and conflict. Make them human. Make them dangerous. Make them emotionally connected to the story. And use ChatGPT to explore all the angles, layer the psychology, and punch up the dialogue until they leap off the page. When done right, your villain won't just challenge your protagonist—they'll captivate your reader. And that's what makes a story unforgettable.

How to Build a Supporting Cast That Matters

Every great protagonist needs a great supporting cast. These are the friends, rivals, love interests, mentors, and wildcards who fill out your story world and give your main character someone to talk to, learn from, lean on, or go up against. But more importantly, a meaningful supporting cast brings emotional depth, narrative balance, and thematic richness to your story. If you're writing a fiction book in one day with ChatGPT, creating a memorable ensemble doesn't have to take hours. With the right approach and smart prompts, you can build an entire cast of compelling characters in minutes—and more importantly, make sure each one actually matters to the story.

The first step is understanding what "supporting" really means. It doesn't mean filler characters who show up for a scene and then vanish. It means people who serve a function. Characters who influence your protagonist's journey. Ask yourself what kind of pressure, reflection, or connection your protagonist needs as they move through their story. Do they need a loyal best friend who keeps them grounded? A cunning rival who constantly pushes them to the edge? A romantic interest who challenges their beliefs? Every side character should exist for a reason—and if they don't, it's okay to cut them loose.

Start by asking ChatGPT something like, "What are five types of supporting characters that could challenge or complement a protagonist who's a reclusive genius?" This will give you suggestions like a carefree roommate who forces the protagonist into social situations, or a skeptical detective who suspects them of something. From there, you can tweak personalities, motivations, and roles to fit your story. The goal is to create contrast and connection—characters who either reflect parts of the protagonist or bring out parts they're trying to avoid.

One trick that works really well is assigning each supporting character a *function* in your protagonist's arc. For example, the mentor might represent the path of wisdom and restraint. The rival might embody unchecked ambition. The love interest could challenge your main character's emotional walls. The antagonist might not even be the main villain—but someone who believes the opposite of what your hero stands for. Use ChatGPT to help define these roles: "Give me character archetypes that complement a protagonist learning to trust others again." You'll get a list of emotionally resonant possibilities you can start building into the cast.

Once you've chosen your key supporting characters, give them goals of their own. They don't exist just to prop up the protagonist—they have their own motivations, their own pasts, and their own internal conflicts. This is what makes them feel real. You can prompt ChatGPT with, "Create a backstory and goal for a secondary character who is hiding something from the protagonist," and suddenly your side character has layers. Maybe they're helping, but for the wrong reasons. Maybe they're sabotaging things because they're afraid of losing the protagonist. Complexity is the key to memorability.

Voice is another huge part of making your cast stand out. If everyone talks and thinks the same way, the story goes flat. Ask ChatGPT to help distinguish them: "Give each of these four characters a unique voice, tone, and way of speaking." You'll get dialogue examples that show how one character might use dry wit, another rambles nervously, another speaks in clipped, confident bursts. Those differences add texture to your scenes and help the reader immediately recognize who's speaking—even without name tags.

Relationships between supporting characters matter too. It's not just how they connect with the protagonist—it's how they interact with each other. That's where you find natural tension, humor, and depth. You can say to ChatGPT, "Describe the dynamic between a bitter mentor and an idealistic rookie who both care about the protagonist," and you'll get a set of interactions that go beyond the main character's perspective. The story begins to feel like a living world, not just a series of scenes propped up around your lead.

Supporting characters also give you opportunities to reinforce your themes. If your story is about redemption, then each side character might represent a different belief about whether people can truly change. One might be proof that change is possible. Another might be bitterly skeptical. A third might be in the middle, unsure which way to lean. These thematic reflections make your story feel tighter and more meaningful. Ask ChatGPT, "How can I use my supporting cast to explore the theme of identity?" and you'll get a roadmap of subtle narrative echoes.

Sometimes a side character becomes the secret weapon of your story. They steal scenes. They deliver the funniest lines, the most brutal truths, or the quietest emotional moments. This often happens when you give them freedom to be unexpected. Maybe the nervous assistant turns out to be a genius. Maybe the cheerful best friend has a dark secret. Maybe the comic relief has the most profound insight in the whole book. ChatGPT can help generate character quirks and reversals: "Give me three surprising twists for a secondary character who seems harmless at first." Suddenly, your ensemble cast becomes a source of fresh momentum.

You should also consider where each supporting character enters and exits the story. Don't overload the first chapter with too many names. Introduce characters gradually, when they're needed. If you're writing fast, it's easy to throw in characters just to fill space—but later, they can feel like clutter. ChatGPT can help you structure the timing: "When is the best point in a story to introduce a mentor figure who will later betray the protagonist?" It'll give you guidance on pacing and presence, so each character lands at the right time.

And of course, every supporting character needs a purpose in the plot. Even if it's small. They should influence something. Save the hero. Delay them. Offer a key piece of information. Become a problem. Solve one. You can use prompts like, "Give me plot functions for a supporting character who only appears in the second act," and get a list of ideas that help them matter without taking over.

Once you've created your cast, make a quick reference list: name, role, personality, goal, connection to protagonist, and key moments. It doesn't have to be long—just a sentence or two each. ChatGPT can format this for you too. This cheat sheet helps you keep characters consistent as you write, especially when you're drafting fast and don't have time to scroll back through earlier scenes.

A great supporting cast brings your story to life. They test the protagonist. They add humor, tension, and heart. They reveal sides of your main character that you can't show in a vacuum. And most importantly, they make your world feel bigger than just one person's journey. With ChatGPT by your side, you can build a cast of characters who all have something to say—and something to do. They'll each matter in the story, and to the reader. And when that happens, your one-day novel won't just feel complete—it'll feel full of people we want to spend time with, even after the final page.

Mapping Out Character Arcs with AI

One of the most powerful things a story can offer is transformation. Watching a character change—or resist change—across the length of a book is what gives a story its emotional depth and sense of purpose. This transformation, whether it's internal, relational, or philosophical, is known as a character arc. When you're writing a fiction book in a single day with ChatGPT, plotting a strong character arc quickly might seem like a stretch. But with the right prompts and structure, you can map out meaningful and believable arcs for every major character in your story in under an hour. And when you do, your book goes from a sequence of events to a deeply human journey.

Let's start with your protagonist. The first step in designing their arc is understanding where they begin and where they end—not just in terms of location or circumstance, but emotionally and psychologically. You can give ChatGPT a starting point and an endpoint and let it fill in the transformation. Try something like, "Help me map a character arc for a woman who starts off afraid of intimacy and ends up sacrificing her safety to protect someone she loves." The model will outline emotional beats, key scenes, and choices that reflect that inner change.

A strong character arc often revolves around a lie the character believes about themselves or the world, and the truth they gradually uncover. Maybe they believe they're unworthy of love. Maybe they think vulnerability is weakness. Maybe they assume that people can't change. As the story unfolds, experience and conflict chip away at that lie until they're forced to face a deeper truth. You can ask ChatGPT, "What's a good internal lie for a protagonist who's outwardly successful but emotionally empty?" and get a whole list of possibilities that instantly give your story emotional shape.

Once you know the emotional trajectory, start plotting turning points. These are the key moments that challenge the character's beliefs, confront them with choices, or force them to reckon with their fears. You can ask ChatGPT, "What are five emotional turning points that could shape this arc?" and you'll get beats like "the protagonist betrays someone to protect themselves," or "they see someone else make a brave choice they couldn't make," or "they confess something for the first time and are met with unexpected compassion." These are the scenes that make your character feel real and alive.

The arc doesn't have to be linear, either. In fact, most great arcs include setbacks, regressions, and contradictions. A character might take a big step forward emotionally, then stumble backward in fear. These ups and downs mirror real life and create drama. Ask ChatGPT, "What are some believable setbacks for a character learning to let go of control?" and you'll get small and large ways to make the arc feel earned. This keeps the story engaging because the reader never feels like the transformation is too easy.

You can also map arcs for your supporting cast. These don't have to be as detailed as the protagonist's, but giving your major side characters even a small arc adds richness to your story. Maybe your rival character starts out antagonistic but grows into a reluctant ally. Maybe the mentor character starts off wise and composed but cracks under pressure. Ask ChatGPT, "Give me a mini character arc for a comic relief character who wants to be taken seriously," and you'll get a narrative thread that makes that character more than just a punchline.

If you're working with multiple arcs at once—say, for a love story or ensemble piece—you can map how arcs intersect. Character A's growth might trigger or block Character B's. Their arcs might mirror each other, contrast, or collide. Ask ChatGPT, "How can two characters' arcs affect each other in a story about betrayal and forgiveness?" and you'll get dynamic ideas for building layered, interconnected relationships.

It's also helpful to use structure to frame the arc. Many writers use the three-act story structure, but character arcs have a structure too. There's the Setup (where we see who they are and what they believe), the Catalyst (where something challenges that belief), the Struggle (where they resist or test the new truth), the Revelation (where they accept the truth), and the Change (where they act on it). You can give ChatGPT a character and say, "Help me outline this arc using that five-beat structure," and it will help you plot clear emotional progress through the story.

And don't forget that not all arcs are positive. Some characters fall. They become more bitter, selfish, or closed off. Others refuse to change at all, which in itself becomes the arc—a tragedy of potential left unfulfilled. Ask ChatGPT, "What would a negative character arc look like for a protagonist who starts off idealistic?" and you'll get steps like betrayal, compromise, disillusionment, and eventual corruption. This kind of arc is powerful when you want to tell a story with moral complexity.

Once you have your arc(s), keep a simple summary nearby as you write. One sentence for each major change point is often enough: "Starts off distrustful," "Learns to open up after being helped," "Fails and lashes out," "Finds courage in protecting someone else," "Lets go of fear and acts selflessly." You can even ask ChatGPT to organize this into a chart or bullet list for quick reference while you draft. That way, every scene you write serves the arc—and every moment pushes your character toward or away from who they're meant to become.

Your character's arc is where the real meaning of your story lives. Plot is what happens. Arc is *why it matters*. And with ChatGPT, you don't have to spend days figuring it out. You just need to know who your character is, who they could become, and what stands in their way. The AI can help you connect those dots with scene ideas, emotional logic, and thematic support that fits your story and writing style.

So before you dive into the next chapter of your book, take a little time to shape your character's arc. Ask yourself what truth they need to face. What lie they need to let go of. What choices will define them. And then let ChatGPT help you build a journey that feels rich, powerful, and honest. Because no matter how fast you write your book, if the characters grow, the story will stay with your reader long after the last page.

Dialogue That Sounds Real and Feels Right

If there's one thing that can sink a story faster than a plot hole, it's bad dialogue. You know it when you see it—characters who talk like robots, monologue like philosophers, or deliver exposition like they're reading off a script. Stilted dialogue pulls readers out of the moment, breaks the emotional flow, and makes even the most gripping plot feel fake. But when dialogue sounds real and feels right, it does something magical. It makes characters breathe. It makes relationships come alive. And it turns a simple scene into something unforgettable. The best part? With ChatGPT on your side, writing natural, emotionally charged dialogue becomes way easier—and way more fun.

The first rule of great dialogue is this: real doesn't mean boring. People often assume "realistic" means copying how people talk in everyday life. But in real life, we ramble, repeat ourselves, throw in "ums" and "likes," and drift off mid-sentence. That's fine at the coffee shop, but on the page, it needs to be tighter, sharper, more purposeful. The trick is to *feel* real without getting bogged down by the messiness of actual speech. You want your characters to sound like real people, but real people who've been edited for clarity, rhythm, and dramatic tension.

One great way to achieve this is by giving each character a distinct voice. Your characters shouldn't all sound like you. They should sound like *them.* A weary cop shouldn't speak like a fast-talking teenager. A snarky hacker shouldn't sound like a reserved schoolteacher. Ask ChatGPT for help defining character voices. Try, "Give me three different character voices for a shy librarian, an overconfident con artist, and a jaded war veteran." Then test how those voices affect dialogue. A good voice has rhythm, vocabulary, attitude, and emotional undercurrents. It's not just what they say—it's how they say it.

Dialogue also needs to serve a purpose. It should reveal character, move the plot forward, or increase tension. If it's not doing one of those things, it probably doesn't need to be there. You can ask ChatGPT, "What's a meaningful conversation between two characters who disagree about how to handle a crisis?" and it'll generate an exchange where emotions and goals clash. These are the kinds of scenes that crackle with energy—because the characters want different things and are pushing against each other in words.

Subtext is where good dialogue becomes great. That's when characters *don't* say exactly what they mean, but the meaning is still clear to the reader. It's the tension under the words. The polite smile hiding resentment. The joke masking insecurity. The silence that says everything. If you're stuck making dialogue sound too on-the-nose, ask ChatGPT, "Rewrite this conversation with more subtext and emotional tension," and it'll give you something less direct, more layered, and far more compelling.

Pauses and interruptions can also make dialogue feel more natural. People don't talk in perfect blocks. They trail off, interrupt each other, repeat things, or react mid-sentence. Ask ChatGPT for help with that too: "Make this dialogue more conversational and include natural pauses or hesitations." It might add lines like, "Wait—are you serious?" or "I mean... look, it's not that simple." These subtle beats mimic real human conversation and make the scene feel alive.

The emotional tone of your dialogue should match the context. A fight should feel tense and messy. A romantic moment should feel vulnerable and raw. A joke should actually be funny—or at least lighthearted. If you're unsure about the tone, just describe the scene to ChatGPT: "Two ex-lovers meet by accident at a funeral. One wants to talk, the other doesn't. Write their brief exchange with underlying tension and regret." You'll get a snippet that balances words, silence, and implied emotion. From there, you can adjust the pacing, add beats of action, and shape it to your style.

Sometimes you need dialogue to deliver information—but nobody likes an info dump. The secret is to hide the exposition in conflict, humor, or emotion. Don't just have one character explain something. Have them *reluctantly* explain it. Have another character interrupt or challenge them. Make it part of an argument or a moment of bonding. If you need to deliver backstory, ask ChatGPT, "How can I reveal this information through dialogue without it sounding forced?" and it'll offer naturalistic ways to weave it in.

Another way to write strong dialogue is to let characters speak *past* each other. People often don't listen—they wait to respond. In scenes where emotions run high, let the characters misunderstand each other, deflect, or bring up things that weren't part of the conversation. It creates tension and realism. You can even ask ChatGPT, "Write a scene where two characters are arguing, but neither of them is really hearing the other," and watch the sparks fly.

If your scene has more than two people, think about how each voice plays off the others. Triangular dynamics—two people against one, or one trying to mediate—are rich with opportunity. Group dialogue should feel messy but readable, with each person having a reason to be in the scene and a voice that cuts through the noise. Ask ChatGPT, "Give me a scene where three characters debate a risky plan, each with different priorities," and you'll get the kind of natural, layered group exchange that reveals character through conflict.

Don't forget rhythm. Good dialogue has flow. It's almost musical. Short lines can create tension or urgency. Longer ones can slow things down and deepen emotion. If a scene feels flat, try trimming or rearranging the lines. Or ask ChatGPT, "Rewrite this scene to quicken the pace and heighten tension." You might find that just changing sentence length or moving beats around gives the dialogue a completely new energy.

Finally, read your dialogue out loud. Seriously. You'll hear when something sounds awkward or stiff. If you stumble while reading it, your reader probably will too. You can even read it to ChatGPT and ask, "Does this conversation feel natural? What could improve it?" You'll get specific notes about word choice, pacing, and tone. It's like having an editor sitting next to you—but one who works instantly and never gets tired.

In a one-day writing sprint, dialogue can be your best friend or your worst enemy. It can suck up hours if you get stuck trying to make a conversation sound right. Or it can become the engine of your story, letting characters reveal themselves, relationships evolve, and emotional truths come to the surface—all through what's said and unsaid. With ChatGPT, you've got an endless stream of dialogue practice, guidance, and polish at your fingertips.

So as you write today, lean into conversation. Let your characters speak. Let them interrupt, joke, plead, accuse, confess. And if something sounds off, don't panic—just tell ChatGPT what kind of energy you're going for and let it help you find the right words. Because when the dialogue sounds real and feels right, everything else in the story starts to sing.

Giving Each Character a Unique Voice

If all your characters sound the same, your story runs the risk of feeling flat—no matter how exciting the plot is. Readers may not be able to tell who's talking without a name tag, and worse, they won't believe these are different people living in your world. Voice is one of the most important tools in a writer's kit, and when done right, it gives every character a distinct personality that comes through loud and clear—without needing stage directions or excessive description. The good news is that when you're writing your book in a day with ChatGPT, crafting distinct voices for each character doesn't have to take forever. It can be quick, intuitive, and even fun.

Let's start by getting clear on what we mean by "voice." We're not just talking about accents or slang, although those can play a part. A character's voice includes their rhythm, vocabulary, attitude, worldview, and emotional filter. Do they speak in clipped, direct sentences? Do they ramble and over-explain? Are they sarcastic, poetic, formal, impulsive? Are they guarded or open, optimistic or cynical, warm or cold? These traits shape the way they talk—and the way readers experience them.

You can start with a character's personality and build out from there. Ask ChatGPT something like, "Give me a character voice for a confident but deeply insecure crime boss," or "How would a painfully shy teenager express herself in conversation?" You'll get examples of how they might speak, what kinds of phrases they'd use, and how their emotional state leaks into their words. Once you've got a sample, try writing a paragraph of dialogue in their voice, then have ChatGPT compare it with how another character might say the same thing. This is a quick way to see just how different your voices really are.

Another way to build unique voices is to give each character a "verbal fingerprint." Maybe one character always uses analogies. Another might avoid contractions and speak very precisely. Someone else might swear a lot, but only when nervous. Or they might call everyone "darling" or end sentences with "you know?" These quirks add flavor and make the voice instantly recognizable. Ask ChatGPT, "What are some distinctive speech patterns for a street-smart hustler vs. an old-school professor?" and you'll get unique speech traits you can apply consistently throughout your story.

Voice also comes from a character's background—where they're from, what they do, how much education they've had, what kind of people they've been surrounded by. A character raised in the military might speak in commands. A child of poets might speak in images. You can use this background to shape voice naturally. Try prompts like, "What would the dialogue of a nurse raised in a small town but now working in a chaotic city ER sound like?" The results will suggest how culture, career, and class all influence tone, word choice, and delivery.

Emotion plays a big part too. Characters don't talk the same way when they're scared, angry, in love, or trying to hide something. You can feed scenes into ChatGPT and ask, "Rewrite this dialogue to reflect more desperation and frustration," or "How would this sound if the character were trying to stay calm but was really panicking inside?" Suddenly, the voice isn't just about personality—it's about current emotional reality. This adds richness and variation, even within the same character's voice across different scenes.

Another great technique is to contrast character voices in conversation. A fast-talking optimist and a blunt realist will naturally clash, creating tension and texture. If you write a scene where three characters are discussing the same issue, but each one has a totally different way of expressing themselves, the scene becomes dynamic and layered. Ask ChatGPT, "Write a conversation between a hopeful dreamer, a jaded cynic, and a neutral mediator discussing whether to take a dangerous opportunity." You'll see how voice affects rhythm, tone, and energy—and how it can keep dialogue feeling fresh.

When writing fast, it's easy to let your own authorial voice seep into all your characters. That's fine at first, but as you go back through your draft, look at each line of dialogue and ask, "Could only this character have said that?" If the answer is no, tweak it. Use ChatGPT to revise lines with more character-specific flavor. "Make this sound more impulsive," or "Add some arrogance to this reply," or "Rewrite this like it's coming from someone who's quietly furious." You don't have to guess—just guide the AI with emotion or attitude, and it'll help you shape the tone.

Internal monologue is another chance to differentiate voice. If you're writing in first person or close third, the narration should also reflect the character's thoughts, biases, and internal rhythm. Their fears, humor, guilt, and self-image should show up in how they interpret the world. A paranoid character might describe a sunny day as suspiciously quiet. An optimist might focus on the breeze. Ask ChatGPT, "What would a hopeless romantic think during a tense silence on a first date?" and you'll get insight into how even silence can be filtered through a unique emotional lens.

Let's not forget the silent characters—the ones who speak less or not at all. Voice also comes through action, body language, and what's left unsaid. A character who avoids eye contact and gives short answers might still have a strong voice if their silence speaks volumes. You can use ChatGPT to build this type of presence too: "How can a quiet, stoic character still express themselves powerfully in a scene with no words?" You'll get physical cues, subtle behaviors, and interaction styles that help keep the voice consistent even without spoken lines.

For long-form writing, especially when you're rushing through a one-day book, it helps to keep a "voice map" handy. Just a quick guide with each major character's key traits, common phrases, emotional filters, and speaking patterns. ChatGPT can even generate this for you: "Create a voice reference chart for my five main characters with notes on how each one speaks, what they care about, and what emotional tone colors their dialogue." You can glance at this as you write to keep everyone distinct and consistent.

In the end, giving each character a unique voice is what turns a cast of names into living, breathing people. It makes scenes come alive, makes conversations crackle with energy, and keeps readers engaged because they know exactly who's talking—even without being told. It's not about accents or gimmicks. It's about personality, emotion, and perspective. And with ChatGPT ready to riff with you on tone, rewrite lines for nuance, and help you brainstorm quirks and rhythms, there's no reason your characters can't each speak with their own unmistakable voice.

So before you dive into your next chapter, take a moment to tune in to your cast. Hear them. Let them speak in ways that only they would. Ask for help fine-tuning their voices when needed. Because when each character sounds like themselves—and only themselves—your story doesn't just move. It *resonates*.

How to Use ChatGPT to Write Show-Stopping Scenes

Every great book has those moments—the kind that stop you in your tracks, leave you breathless, and stay with you long after you've turned the page. These show-stopping scenes are where the story peaks emotionally, dramatically, or visually. Maybe it's a character's grand confession. Maybe it's a brutal betrayal. Maybe it's the moment when everything falls apart—or comes together. These scenes are the reason we write and the reason readers keep going. And when you're writing an entire fiction book in one day with ChatGPT, being able to craft show-stopping scenes quickly is an absolute superpower.

Let's start with what makes a scene "show-stopping." It's not just action or drama. It's emotional weight. It's tension that's been building. It's characters making impossible choices, revealing deep truths, or doing something totally unexpected that's also totally earned. These scenes change the story—or the character. They shift momentum. They hit hard because they feel inevitable and yet shocking. And with ChatGPT as your creative partner, you can build these moments layer by layer, and fast.

First, you want to identify which moments in your story are candidates for show-stoppers. Typically, these include the inciting incident, the midpoint twist, the emotional or moral low point, the climax, and the resolution. These are the scenes where something big happens—something that alters the course of the narrative or the trajectory of a character. Ask ChatGPT, "Based on my story outline, which scenes should be the most emotionally or narratively impactful?" It'll point you toward the turning points that deserve that extra attention.

Once you've selected your target scenes, you need to start by anchoring them in emotion. What's the emotional truth of the moment? Is it fear, grief, rage, desperation, love, relief, betrayal? Ask ChatGPT, "How can I write a scene where a character feels relieved and devastated at the same time?" The AI will help you unpack the emotional complexity, layering in details that go beyond just dialogue or action. Because a show-stopping scene doesn't just move the plot forward—it grabs the reader by the heart.

Pacing is crucial here. These scenes often slow time down. They stretch out beats, heighten details, and focus on sensory input. The character isn't just running—they feel their lungs burn, their heartbeat pounding, the taste of copper in their mouth. Ask ChatGPT, "Help me describe a high-stakes moment with intense physical and emotional detail," and you'll get suggestions that make the scene visceral. The goal is to immerse the reader fully, to make them feel like they're *inside* the moment, not just reading about it.

You also want to use contrast. A show-stopping scene hits harder when it breaks the pattern. If your story's been quiet and reflective, a sudden burst of chaos will jolt the reader. If it's been intense and fast-paced, a pause for raw vulnerability can cut deep. You can even prompt ChatGPT with, "How can I use contrast to make a romantic confession in a violent setting more impactful?" and watch how the tension between the two tones creates dramatic friction.

Dialogue in these scenes should be sharp, loaded, and stripped of filler. It's not the time for small talk. Every word should reveal something—whether it's truth, intent, pain, or desire. You can write a draft and ask ChatGPT to sharpen it: "Rewrite this scene to heighten the emotional stakes in the dialogue," or "Make this confrontation more explosive but keep it grounded in the characters' relationship." These tweaks can turn a decent moment into something unforgettable.

Action matters too. In a show-stopping scene, what a character *does* often speaks louder than what they say. A glance. A punch. A kiss. Walking away instead of screaming. Collapsing into silence instead of fighting back. Ask ChatGPT, "What subtle actions could show a character is heartbroken but trying to appear composed?" and you'll get behavior-driven cues that speak volumes without a word being spoken. This is how you create tension that hums on the page.

Another ingredient is unpredictability. A show-stopping scene should surprise the reader—but not confuse them. It should make perfect sense in hindsight, even if they didn't see it coming. If you need help twisting the moment, ask ChatGPT, "What unexpected choice could a character make in this scene that still feels emotionally honest?" The answer might give your plot a fresh turn and elevate the scene into something no one saw coming—but everyone remembers.

Don't forget about silence and space. Sometimes, the most powerful part of a scene is what's *not* said. The breath between words. The silence after a question. The weight of someone walking out without answering. ChatGPT can help with that, too. Prompt it with, "Add beats of silence and physical detail to this scene to increase tension," and it'll show you how to stretch moments just enough to make them ache.

If your scene is visual and cinematic—like a final battle, a massive reveal, or a surreal dream sequence—focus on visual rhythm. What does the reader *see* second by second? What's the dominant color, texture, or movement? Try something like, "Help me write a slow-motion action sequence with emotional resonance," and ChatGPT will suggest ways to combine poetic language with sharp imagery to create a truly immersive moment.

And finally, cap it off with consequence. A show-stopping scene changes something. If it doesn't leave the character altered—or the reader reeling—it's not quite there yet. After you write your big moment, ask, "What are the immediate and emotional consequences of this scene, and how will it change the direction of the story?" Let ChatGPT help you figure out what happens next. That way, the impact of the moment isn't just in the scene—it ripples through the entire book.

When you're writing a novel in a day, you don't have time to second-guess every sentence. But you *do* have time to stop and give a few scenes the extra care they need to shine. With ChatGPT, you can write a solid version of the moment, get help enhancing it, and polish the language all in one sitting. It's like having a writing partner who helps you swing for the fences—and connect.

So go ahead—pick your big moments. Think emotionally. Think visually. Think dramatically. Then let ChatGPT help you layer, sharpen, stretch, and explode those scenes until they don't just work... they stop the show. Because when your story has a few moments that hit like lightning, readers forgive almost anything else. And they'll remember your book for the way it made them *feel.* 18. The Art of Scene Transitions with AI Assistance

The Art of Scene Transitions with AI Assistance

Scene transitions are one of those subtle elements of storytelling that, when done well, are nearly invisible. But when done poorly, they're jarring, awkward, and can break the flow of even the most gripping story. Transitions are the connective tissue between scenes. They're what help the reader move from one moment, location, or character's point of view to another without getting confused, lost, or pulled out of the emotional rhythm. When you're writing an entire fiction book in one day using ChatGPT, smooth transitions become your best friend. They keep the story flowing and allow you to shift gears without stalling your momentum.

A scene transition doesn't need to be flashy or over-explained. In fact, it's usually best when it simply slides the reader from one beat to the next. The trick is to maintain continuity of tone, emotion, or theme. Whether you're jumping forward in time, cutting to another character, or shifting to a new setting, there has to be a reason for the shift, and the transition should reflect that. This is where ChatGPT becomes incredibly useful. You can describe your two scenes and ask, "How can I transition from this emotional confrontation to a quiet reflective moment the next morning?" and it will help you bridge the gap with a sentence or two that eases the reader across the change.

There are several types of scene transitions, and knowing how to use each one can give you a lot of variety in your writing. The most basic is the *time jump.* Maybe a day has passed, or an hour, or several years. Rather than launching into a time stamp, you can show the change through environmental cues, mood, or small actions. Ask ChatGPT, "How do I show that a week has passed without breaking the emotional tone of the last scene?" and it will give you natural transitions that reflect time slipping forward through character thoughts, setting descriptions, or physical changes.

Another common transition is the *location shift.* You're in one place, and now the story moves elsewhere. The key here is to orient the reader quickly but organically. You don't need a GPS update—just something to ground the new setting in mood, sensory detail, or emotional contrast. For example, if the last scene ends with a tense argument in a cramped apartment, and the next opens in a peaceful meadow, the transition should acknowledge the shift in tone. You can ask ChatGPT, "Help me write a seamless location transition that contrasts tension with calm," and it will generate a paragraph that makes the change feel purposeful.

Character perspective shifts are another place where transitions really matter. If your story is told through multiple viewpoints, each switch needs to feel earned, not random. You want to time the shift so that one character's moment of insight, crisis, or inaction leads naturally into the other's. Ask ChatGPT, "Write a transition that shifts from the protagonist's point of view to the antagonist's without losing narrative flow," and you'll get something that ties the emotional beats together. Often, you can echo a line of thought, an object, or a theme across the perspectives to create that seamless handoff.

Sometimes, you'll want to *cut sharply* between scenes for dramatic effect. That's okay too—but even a hard cut benefits from a sense of rhythm. It might come in the form of a powerful last line, a silence, or a line of dialogue that sets up the next moment. ChatGPT is really good at this. You can say, "Give me a punchy last line that sets up the next chapter, where everything changes," and it'll offer options that land like a beat in a movie. These lines help end one scene with a purpose and prime the reader for what comes next.

Transitions can also work thematically. Let's say your last scene is about loss, and the next is about rebirth or hope. You can thread an image, color, or metaphor across the transition to give the shift symbolic weight. Ending with a character staring out a rainy window, and opening the next scene with sunshine breaking through clouds, is an old trick—but it works because it signals the emotional tone without spelling it out. You can ask ChatGPT, "Suggest a symbolic transition between a funeral scene and a moment of new beginnings," and it'll give you language that bridges mood and meaning.

If your story has fast-paced sequences—like action, suspense, or thriller beats—you'll want quick, clean transitions that keep the reader moving without confusion. These can be as simple as a line break and a short sentence. "Three hours later, he was bleeding on the floor of the warehouse." Done. Or, if you want something with more style, ChatGPT can help you punch it up: "Write a gritty, high-energy transition between a quiet planning scene and an ambush." You'll get options that maintain urgency and tone.

Sometimes transitions don't happen between *scenes*, but *within* a scene. A character goes from past to present in their thoughts. The setting shifts slightly. The mood swings. These micro-transitions matter too. They help the scene feel dynamic instead of static. You can say, "Help me write a smooth emotional shift from curiosity to fear in a scene where the protagonist discovers a hidden door," and ChatGPT will help you map the subtle beat changes that make the scene feel alive.

A great way to practice this is to write a few key sentences yourself and then ask ChatGPT to refine them. Say, "I want to go from a romantic rooftop moment to a harsh interrogation room. Here's what I've got. Can you smooth this out?" You'll get a version that connects the emotional undertones, adds rhythm, and guides the reader along without making them trip. This saves you time and energy—two things you need to preserve when writing your book in a single day.

You can also treat transitions as mini-cliffhangers. End a scene with an unanswered question, an unexpected sound, or a character making a sudden decision. That pulls the reader into the next scene almost automatically. Ask ChatGPT, "What's a good transitional hook to go from a character discovering a secret to confronting the person who's been hiding it?" and you'll get something that's not just a bridge—it's a pull.

If you want to keep your transitions consistent in tone and style, you can even ask ChatGPT to generate a series of them based on your chapter outline. "Give me short, thematic transitions between these 10 chapter beats," and you'll get connective phrases that make the story feel unified, like each part flows naturally into the next.

So while transitions may seem like the glue between the good stuff, don't underestimate how powerful they are. A well-written transition keeps the reader immersed, reinforces mood, and sharpens the pacing. With ChatGPT, you can smooth out rough edges, find poetic or punchy ways to link scenes, and keep your narrative energy high without getting bogged down in logistics. Think of it like film editing—cutting, fading, dissolving, or smashing to the next scene with intent. That's the art. And now, thanks to AI, you don't have to do it alone—or slow down your writing sprint to make it work.

Using ChatGPT to Set the Mood and Atmosphere

Mood and atmosphere are the secret spices that give your story flavor. They're not about what happens but *how it feels*. You can write two identical scenes—a character walking into a room, for example—and depending on how you craft the mood, one could feel warm and inviting, while the other could drip with dread. That's the power of atmosphere. It's the emotional weather of your story, and it affects how every word lands with the reader. When you're writing a fiction book in one day with ChatGPT, mastering this element quickly and effectively is a massive advantage. You can use the AI to help you establish tone, maintain it across chapters, and shift it at just the right moments for emotional impact.

Mood is the emotional current that runs beneath a scene. It's created by your choice of language, pacing, imagery, and even sentence structure. Atmosphere is closely related—it's the sensory and environmental setup that supports that mood. Together, they turn your scenes from "stuff happening" into "experiences that linger." And when you're writing fast, it helps to know you can turn to ChatGPT for quick injections of atmospheric gold, whether you're aiming for eerie, romantic, nostalgic, gritty, whimsical, or anything in between.

Let's say you've got a basic scene. Your character walks into an abandoned house. The plot beat is simple—they're looking for something. But how should the reader feel? Is it suspenseful? Melancholic? Peaceful? Haunted? That's where mood comes in. You can tell ChatGPT, "Describe this abandoned house scene with a tense, horror-like atmosphere," and it will generate details that evoke anxiety: creaking floorboards, broken glass glittering like teeth, cold air brushing against the neck. If you ask instead for a "melancholic, nostalgic atmosphere," you'll get descriptions of faded wallpaper, dusty sunbeams, and the scent of something long gone. The same action—entering the house—becomes a completely different emotional experience.

This technique works scene by scene. Before writing each section of your book, ask yourself: what should this *feel* like? Not what happens, but what emotional tone do you want to wrap the reader in? Once you know that, ask ChatGPT to help you set the stage. For example, "Describe a late-night diner with a lonely, noir-style mood," or "Help me write a summer forest with a sense of childlike wonder." The results can be used directly or tweaked to match your style, but they'll give you a tone to write into—and save you time guessing at the right words.

Tone shifts are another area where ChatGPT excels. Sometimes your story needs to go from light to dark, or calm to chaotic, within a few paragraphs. These transitions can be tricky if you're moving fast. Ask ChatGPT, "Help me shift the mood from peaceful reflection to sudden danger in this scene," and it'll guide the language through that transformation. The key is usually in contrast—taking one sensory or emotional thread and turning it, like a gear grinding into another mood. The sound of rain might go from soothing to ominous. A candle might flicker too hard. A laugh might ring hollow.

Sound, scent, and texture are incredibly effective tools for setting atmosphere. ChatGPT can help you lean into these sensory layers by generating immersive descriptions. You can ask, "Give me sensory details to create a claustrophobic atmosphere in a small room," and get suggestions like stale air, flickering fluorescent lights, the hum of a refrigerator, or the way voices echo too loud off the walls. These cues build immersion quickly and subtly—they help the reader *feel* the scene, not just visualize it.

You can even use ChatGPT to color entire chapters with mood. If your second act is supposed to feel like a slow descent into despair, you can ask, "Suggest imagery, colors, and recurring motifs that could reinforce a tone of creeping hopelessness," and then sprinkle those elements throughout your scenes—gray skies, failing lights, the smell of rot, forgotten places, or echoes that fade before they reach the ear. These recurring atmospheric touches create emotional consistency, even when the plot shifts.

Mood can also be reflected in the protagonist's internal experience. Sometimes the atmosphere isn't about the setting at all—it's about how your character *perceives* the setting. ChatGPT can help you write through that emotional filter. Ask, "Describe a busy street as it would appear to someone who is grieving," and you'll get a version of the scene that's hollow, distant, and disconnected. Now try the same scene for someone who just fell in love, and you'll get warmth, color, and an overwhelming sense of life. You're using the same backdrop, but showing it through two different emotional lenses.

If your story includes moments of horror, suspense, or dread, you can use ChatGPT to help build slow-burn tension. Say, "Write a scene that begins ordinary but slowly becomes unsettling," and the AI will gradually tweak the language—adding eerie details, breaking the rhythm, inserting sounds or silences that suggest something's off. It's like having a pacing assistant who knows how to stretch tension and then snap it when the moment's right.

On the flip side, for joyful or romantic scenes, ChatGPT can help dial up the atmosphere without tipping into cliché. Ask, "Help me write a romantic scene with a whimsical tone that doesn't feel cheesy," and you'll get soft metaphors, gentle rhythms, and sweet-but-grounded detail. It's a quick way to hit the emotional tone you want, especially when you're pressed for time and need the scene to land immediately.

You can also use mood and atmosphere to reflect your story's themes. If your book is about isolation, the settings might all feel vast, echoing, or emotionally distant. If it's about transformation, you might use weather, seasons, or light as metaphor. ChatGPT can help with that too. Try, "Suggest setting details to reinforce a theme of personal transformation," and it might offer things like melting ice, shifting shadows, or mirrors that crack and reflect distorted images. These aren't just mood tricks—they're thematic devices disguised as description.

As you move through your one-day writing sprint, keep a note open with the tone goals for each chapter. You can even label each one with a mood: "Chapter 3: tense and suspicious. Chapter 4: bittersweet nostalgia. Chapter 5: dreamlike unease." Then use ChatGPT as your atmosphere assistant for each section. Feed it your chapter summary and say, "Infuse this chapter with a mood of fragile hope," and let it suggest descriptions, emotional beats, and tone-aligned language you can drop right into the draft.

Setting mood and atmosphere isn't about showing off flowery writing. It's about creating an emotional environment where the plot can breathe and the reader can feel. With ChatGPT helping you weave that feeling into every scene, you can go deeper, faster, and more effectively—turning your quickly-written novel into an experience that feels rich, layered, and emotionally resonant.

So when the plot is moving, the dialogue is flowing, and the characters are evolving, don't forget to ask: what should this *feel* like right now? Then bring in ChatGPT, load up your scene, and build the emotional weather your story deserves. Because when the mood is right, the magic happens—even if you're writing the whole thing in just one day.

Crafting Settings That Feel Like Characters

There's something unforgettable about a story where the setting doesn't just serve as a backdrop, but feels alive—like another character in the narrative. Think about the eerie Overlook Hotel in *The Shining*, the smoggy, rain-soaked streets of *Blade Runner's* Los Angeles, or the windswept moors in *Wuthering Heights*. These places do more than house the plot; they influence it, shape the characters, and often symbolize something deeper. When you're writing a fiction book in one day with ChatGPT, crafting settings that breathe and interact with your story is a powerful shortcut to immersive storytelling. You don't need pages and pages of description—you just need to treat the world as if it has a soul.

The first shift in mindset is to stop thinking of setting as something static. It's not just "where things happen." It's *how* things happen and *why* people behave the way they do. A city under constant surveillance affects how characters move and speak. A crumbling mansion with locked doors and strange sounds at night influences how they feel and think. When you treat your setting like a character—with moods, reactions, history, and personality—you create depth that seeps into every part of the story.

So how do you build that kind of setting quickly and effectively? Start by deciding what emotional energy the place gives off. Is it warm, cold, threatening, magical, isolating, oppressive, freeing? You can ask ChatGPT, "Describe a small town that feels safe on the surface but is hiding dark secrets," and you'll get atmospheric details that immediately create mood: the too-perfect lawns, the locked library basement, the way everyone smiles just a bit too long. These elements give your setting a vibe. That vibe is what makes it feel like a character.

The next step is to give the setting a *history*. Like a character's backstory, a setting with a past has layers. A house that was once a hospital. A forest that used to be the site of executions. A spaceship that's been adrift for centuries. Even if you don't reveal all that history up front, it will inform how you describe it and how characters respond to it. Ask ChatGPT, "What is a mysterious backstory for an abandoned theater in a post-apocalyptic city?" and you'll get something you can use to deepen the presence of the setting in the reader's mind—even if it's just hinted at through old posters, bullet holes in the curtains, or an echo that never quite fades.

You can also give your setting *quirks and contradictions*, the same way you would with a character. A desert that's unnaturally cold at night. A luxurious palace with a single hallway no one enters. A spaceship that hums like it's breathing. These oddities make the environment memorable and contribute to the feeling that the world itself has personality. Ask ChatGPT for help with this too: "What's a strange feature that could make this castle feel alive?" and see how those odd touches become part of your story's signature atmosphere.

Dialogue with setting is another way to bring it to life. Have your characters react to their environment not just with description, but with emotion and memory. Maybe the smell of jasmine reminds your protagonist of a childhood betrayal. Maybe a storm always hits before something terrible happens, and they brace for it without realizing. You can ask ChatGPT, "Show how a character emotionally responds to returning to a home they once fled," and it will generate interior monologue and reactions that tie the setting to the character's journey.

Another technique is to let your setting *change*. A setting that evolves with the plot mirrors the character arc and keeps the world feeling dynamic. Maybe a haunted house slowly reveals more of itself. Maybe a war-torn city rebuilds, or a dying world blooms again. You can even use the setting as a metaphor for the protagonist's internal transformation. Ask ChatGPT, "How can a deteriorating city reflect a character's emotional unraveling?" and you'll get ideas that turn cracked windows, broken elevators, and fading street signs into visual echoes of what's happening inside your hero.

Sensory detail is your best tool for giving the setting texture. Go beyond the visual. What does the place *smell* like? How does it sound in the quiet? What textures does the character feel underfoot, in their hands, or against their skin? What happens to the air in moments of tension? Ask ChatGPT, "Give me sensory details to describe an underground bunker that feels both safe and suffocating," and the sensory language will pour out—muffled sounds, recycled air, metal walls that sweat in the dark. These details don't just set the scene; they *infuse* it.

You can also let your setting *interact* with the characters. Maybe it resists them—like a forest that seems to close off paths. Maybe it embraces them—like a cozy kitchen that makes them lower their guard. Maybe it mirrors or mocks them—like a crumbling statue in a ruined temple that looks suspiciously like the main character. These interactions create tension or comfort that add another emotional layer to the narrative. Ask ChatGPT, "Write a scene where a setting seems to judge a character silently," and it will offer descriptive cues that add this layer of personality to the world.

Themes can be reinforced through setting too. If your story is about power and corruption, the setting might include tall buildings casting shadows over the poor. If it's about escape, you might write wide open skies, endless roads, or windows that don't quite close. ChatGPT can help: "What kind of setting would enhance a story about personal freedom vs. societal control?" It'll give you architectural cues, social structures, even color palettes that visually and emotionally match your theme.

Naming places is another way to give setting character. Don't just call it "the town" or "the base." Give it a name that tells a story—Stonebridge, Hollow Creek, The Deep Nest. These names create instant associations and add weight. Ask ChatGPT, "Suggest names for a hidden city in the mountains with a tragic history," and you'll get options that evoke tone, mystery, and memory.

In fast writing, it's easy to rush past setting—but when you slow down for just a moment and give the world a little breath, a little thought, it pays off. With ChatGPT, you can explore the soul of your story's environment just as easily as you build your characters. Because when the setting has a voice of its own, when it speaks through shadows, light, texture, history, and metaphor, it stops being background—and becomes part of the story's beating heart.

So next time you write a scene, don't just ask, "Where are they?" Ask, "Who is this place?" Then invite ChatGPT to help you discover the answer. Because when setting becomes character, your story doesn't just take place somewhere—it *belongs* there.

Worldbuilding in Minutes with Prompts

Worldbuilding is one of the most exciting parts of writing fiction—but it can also be a trap. Many writers fall into the black hole of spending weeks designing elaborate kingdoms, political systems, and languages before writing a single line of story. And while that level of detail is great for epic fantasy or sci-fi sagas, when you're trying to write an entire book in a single day, you need a faster, smarter approach. That's where ChatGPT becomes your secret weapon. With the right prompts, you can build rich, textured worlds in just minutes—worlds that feel big enough to hold your story, but focused enough not to slow you down.

The key is to build just enough to support your story—and then layer in details as needed. You're not building the whole planet. You're building the part your characters live in, the rules that shape their choices, and the elements that affect the tone of the story. And you can do all of that by asking the right questions.

Let's say you're writing a sci-fi adventure. Instead of spending hours figuring out orbital mechanics or the entire history of interstellar travel, you can ask ChatGPT, "Give me a brief overview of a spacefaring civilization ruled by corporate dynasties," and within seconds, you'll get a compact framework: who's in charge, what the power struggles look like, what kind of tech is common, and how everyday people live under that system. Boom—setting established. Now you can start writing scenes that feel grounded in a real place.

Or maybe you're writing a fantasy story. You don't need a thousand-year timeline or a full pantheon of gods to start. You just need atmosphere, rules of magic, and a few cultural quirks. Ask ChatGPT, "Describe a mountain city powered by elemental magic, with a council that controls access to water," and you'll get a detailed response you can build scenes around immediately. You can always expand later—but for now, the world feels real enough to explore.

Worldbuilding through prompts is also fantastic for generating political structures, belief systems, social dynamics, and local color. You can focus on what actually shows up in the story. If your character has to sneak through a black-market district, don't worry about the whole economy—ask ChatGPT, "What would a hidden black-market bazaar look like in a futuristic underwater city?" and get quick sensory details, character types, and background lore. You've got what you need for the scene, and it only took a minute.

The beauty of this method is that it's reactive. You're not building the world first and forcing the story to fit. You're letting the story lead, and building the world to support it. If you suddenly realize your character needs to break a major law, ask ChatGPT, "What's an unusual but dangerous crime in this society, and what are the consequences?" Now you've got legal systems, cultural norms, and stakes—all tailored to your plot in real time.

This works brilliantly for smaller world details, too. If your character walks into a tavern, you don't need a fantasy cookbook. Just ask, "What's a strange drink served in a remote jungle village, and how does it taste?" Now you've added a unique cultural detail that makes your world feel alive without slowing you down. Do the same for fashion, slang, weather, architecture, and rituals. You can ask, "What would a mourning ceremony look like in a desert culture that reveres the sun?" and get something deeply atmospheric that reinforces your setting and themes.

Worldbuilding also includes technology and magic systems. Instead of writing an encyclopedia, ask for fast, clear rules. "Give me a simple but unique magic system based on emotions," or "What are the limits of AI in a society where machines govern everything but still need human dreams to process logic?" ChatGPT will give you creative, structured ideas you can use instantly—and adjust on the fly.

And don't forget geography. You can map out your fictional world with prompts like, "Describe a coastal kingdom bordered by haunted woods and known for glassworking." You'll get natural boundaries, economic flavor, and mood all in one go. If you want more control, describe your main setting and ask, "What neighboring regions could create conflict or tension with this location?" Now your world isn't just a dot on a map—it's part of a living, breathing landscape with pressure points and story potential.

If you're working with multiple locations—say, a road-trip novel or a fantasy quest—ask for scene-specific mini-worlds. "Describe a cursed village where time moves backward," or "What would a bustling alien bazaar on a desert moon feel like at midnight?" Each location feels distinct, helps define the tone of its chapter, and gives your characters a meaningful place to react to. These bite-sized settings add depth without overwhelming you with information you'll never use.

Another trick is to let ChatGPT generate local legends, myths, or superstitions. These can be slipped into dialogue or used to foreshadow twists. "What's a local folktale told to children in a remote ice-bound settlement?" can yield eerie or whimsical flavor that makes the setting feel lived-in. Readers don't need full history—they need *texture*. And prompts like this give you the brushstrokes to paint a world that feels textured and true.

For long books or series, you can use ChatGPT to create a quick reference sheet: a short guide to your world's regions, rules, culture, and timeline. Ask, "Summarize this fictional world in under 300 words for internal consistency," and now you've got a cheat sheet to glance at as you draft. It's like worldbuilding with a co-pilot—one who remembers everything and never gets stuck.

In the end, worldbuilding doesn't need to be a massive project that delays your writing. It can be light, fast, reactive, and story-driven. When you use ChatGPT to ask targeted prompts, you're not creating a world for its own sake. You're creating a world that serves your characters, fuels your plot, and delivers emotional resonance in every scene.

So next time you need a new location, a cultural tradition, a political conflict, or a weird creature, don't stop and open a dozen tabs or dig through notebooks. Just type in what you need. Let ChatGPT throw ideas at you. Take what fits. Twist what inspires you. And keep moving. Because the story is the heart of your book—and the world you build around it should make that heart beat louder.

How to Keep Your Story's Pacing Tight

Pacing is what gives your story its heartbeat. It's the rhythm that pulls the reader forward, scene by scene, sentence by sentence, never letting them lose interest or feel like they're stuck waiting for something to happen. In a one-day novel sprint, keeping your pacing tight is essential—not just to finish the book on time, but to make sure the story flows in a way that feels urgent, lean, and alive. When you're writing with ChatGPT, you have an incredible tool at your fingertips for keeping that rhythm sharp and engaging from start to finish.

The first thing to know about pacing is that it's not about speed—it's about *momentum*. A slow scene can still have great pacing if it builds tension, develops character, or deepens the theme. A fast scene can fall flat if it feels rushed, disjointed, or pointless. What you want is *purposeful motion*—each paragraph doing something, each scene pushing the story forward, even if it's quiet, even if it's sad, even if it's just one character sitting alone with their thoughts.

A great way to maintain momentum is to begin each scene with a clear objective. What is the character trying to achieve? What question is being asked, and what's standing in the way? Ask ChatGPT before writing each scene, "What's the core tension or goal in this moment?" and it'll help you focus. That way, the scene has a sense of direction, and you're not meandering through description or dialogue that isn't anchored to anything meaningful.

Transitions between scenes are another place where pacing often drags. If a chapter ends with a character walking away from a confrontation, don't spend the first three paragraphs of the next chapter describing them making tea and thinking about their childhood—unless that childhood is directly tied to the emotional aftermath of the scene. Instead, jump to the next moment of change. ChatGPT can help you bridge that gap. Ask, "Give me a tight transition between an emotional argument and a high-stakes meeting," and you'll get a quick handoff that doesn't lose tension.

One of the fastest ways to tighten your pacing is to trim internal monologue and descriptive excess. Yes, readers like depth—but too much wandering thought can feel like stalling. Use ChatGPT to help you refine these sections. Say, "Rewrite this paragraph to keep the emotional impact but cut the word count by half," and you'll get a tighter version that keeps the punch but loses the fluff. You can do this with entire scenes if they're feeling bloated. Sometimes, less really is more.

Action and dialogue are natural pacing accelerators. If your story is dragging, let characters *do* something. Even a tense conversation can have physical stakes—movement, setting interaction, interruptions. Ask ChatGPT, "How can I turn this static argument into something more dynamic?" and you'll get ideas like pacing the room, throwing something, storming out, or having another character walk in. These little shifts make scenes feel alive.

Scene structure also matters. Keep an eye on how long each chapter or scene runs. If one goes on for pages without a shift in tone, stakes, or energy, you may be overstaying your welcome. ChatGPT can help analyze your structure. Feed it a scene and ask, "What could I cut or rearrange to keep this pacing tighter?" It'll highlight lines or beats that don't serve the momentum.

You can also play with sentence structure. Short sentences speed things up. Long, winding ones slow it down. When you're in the middle of an action sequence or emotionally tense moment, don't be afraid to chop your prose down. Ask ChatGPT, "Rewrite this scene with faster pacing and shorter sentences," and it'll help match the rhythm to the mood. Likewise, when you want to slow things down for emotional impact, ask for help making the language more lyrical or introspective.

Another tip: drop the exposition when the stakes are high. In the middle of a chase, a fight, or a critical decision, don't pause to explain how the engine works or how the character's parents met. Save that for quieter scenes—or better yet, weave it in through implication, dialogue, or brief flashbacks. If you're not sure whether a chunk of exposition is helping or hurting the pacing, ask ChatGPT, "Does this background info slow the scene down? How else could I reveal it?" You'll get suggestions that keep the story moving while still feeding the reader what they need to know.

Pacing also benefits from variety. You don't want every chapter to feel the same length, same structure, same tone. Mix it up. A few rapid-fire scenes followed by a slower, emotionally loaded chapter gives the reader room to breathe and absorb what just happened. ChatGPT can help map that out. Say, "Give me a pacing map for this outline with fast and slow chapters balanced," and you'll get a suggested structure that maintains energy while allowing room for depth.

Don't be afraid to start scenes *late* and end them *early*. That's one of the best tricks for tight pacing. Begin right at the moment of tension or decision—not five minutes before. Finish right after the emotional or narrative payoff—not after the characters talk it to death. If you're not sure where to cut, ask ChatGPT, "Trim this scene to start at the inciting moment and end at the impact." You'll be surprised how much stronger it becomes.

If your story has subplots, be careful not to let them drag the pace. Every subplot should either raise the stakes, deepen the theme, or reflect something in the main plot. If it's just there to fill space, your pacing will suffer. Ask ChatGPT, "How can this subplot connect more directly to the protagonist's arc?" and refine it so it adds tension or relevance rather than distraction.

And finally, use cliffhangers and unanswered questions strategically. You don't have to end every chapter with someone screaming or getting punched, but ending with something unresolved—a secret, a decision, a discovery—pulls the reader into the next page. ChatGPT can help write punchy chapter endings. Try, "Give me three possible last lines for this chapter that would make the reader want to keep going," and you'll get momentum-boosting hooks on demand.

In a one-day novel sprint, you don't have the luxury of meandering. Every scene, every line, every chapter has to count. ChatGPT helps you stay sharp, make decisions fast, and keep the energy high without sacrificing character or meaning. When you learn to master pacing, your story won't just move—it'll fly. And the reader? They'll hold on tight and never look back.

Injecting Tension and Conflict with Every Chapter

Tension is the engine that keeps a reader turning pages. It's not just for action scenes or thrillers—it belongs in *every* genre, and ideally, in *every* chapter. Whether it's a whispered secret, a missed glance, an unspoken fear, or a bomb ticking under the floorboards, tension is what pulls readers forward. Without it, even the most beautifully written scenes fall flat. And when you're writing a full novel in one day with ChatGPT, keeping tension alive in every chapter isn't just a storytelling tool—it's your safety net. It ensures your story doesn't sag, your characters don't drift, and your reader doesn't check out.

Let's start by redefining tension. It doesn't always mean conflict in the dramatic, shouting-match sense. Tension is simply *unresolved energy*. It's a question that hasn't been answered. A feeling that hasn't been expressed. A threat that hasn't been named. When there's something unspoken beneath the dialogue or something looming beyond the next page, the reader feels it, even if they can't quite put their finger on what it is.

Every chapter should carry at least one thread of tension—ideally more. Before you write each chapter, stop and ask: *What's the conflict here?* It doesn't need to be explosive. It could be internal: a character struggling with guilt. It could be relational: two characters avoiding a subject that needs to be discussed. Or it could be situational: a deadline approaching, a secret about to be revealed, or a decision that needs to be made. Ask ChatGPT, "What's a subtle source of tension I can add to this scene?" and you'll get options that work within your existing chapter but add an edge that keeps things interesting.

A useful trick is to insert a question at the start of each chapter that won't be answered until the end—or even later in the book. That question can be as simple as, "Will they say yes?" or as complex as, "Can she trust this new ally?" When you give ChatGPT your chapter outline and ask, "What narrative question can I plant here to keep the tension going?", you're instantly building suspense, even in quieter moments.

Dialogue is one of your sharpest tools for injecting tension. Characters don't need to argue to create conflict. They can talk around something. They can avoid eye contact, change the subject, lie outright, or say the right words in the wrong tone. Ask ChatGPT to help layer this in: "Write a scene where two characters are discussing something ordinary, but one of them is hiding something." The AI will craft responses with a little edge, a pause, a silence—those tiny gaps that make a conversation crackle.

Setting can also add tension, especially when it contrasts with the emotional state of your characters. A peaceful beach can feel ominous if your character is expecting a confrontation. A warm, friendly party can feel suffocating if someone's harboring a secret. Use ChatGPT to shape this mood: "Describe a happy setting with an undercurrent of dread," and you'll get descriptions that serve the story and amplify the tension, even without direct conflict.

Pacing is part of tension, too. If everything in your chapter resolves too neatly, the reader relaxes—and in a novel you're writing fast, you can't afford to let that happen. You don't need to tie up every loose end in every chapter. In fact, it's better if you don't. Let questions linger. Let emotions fester. Let promises go unfulfilled. Use ChatGPT to help you hold that space: "Rewrite this chapter ending with a cliffhanger or unresolved emotional beat," and suddenly you've got forward motion into the next part of the story.

Character conflict is your tension lifeline. Even if the external plot is quiet for a bit, your characters should want different things, misunderstand each other, or clash over how to move forward. Ask ChatGPT, "Give me a small but meaningful disagreement between these two characters," and it'll offer friction that feels organic. These little sparks are what light the fire of great drama—they don't have to be explosive, but they should be real.

Another great way to add tension is to layer in *dramatic irony*—when the reader knows something the character doesn't. This creates delicious tension because we're waiting for the moment of discovery. Let's say the reader knows there's a traitor in the group, but the protagonist doesn't. Ask ChatGPT, "How can I build dramatic irony in a scene without giving too much away?" and it will help you walk that line—teasing the reveal, building anxiety, and keeping the reader on edge.

Foreshadowing is another sneaky way to inject tension. A single line—"He wouldn't realize the truth until it was far too late"—can make an otherwise ordinary chapter feel charged with potential danger. Ask ChatGPT, "Add subtle foreshadowing to this calm scene," and you'll get breadcrumbs you can scatter through the prose, building subconscious pressure in your reader's mind.

Let's talk about stakes. Tension without stakes is just noise. Your characters have to care. The reader has to know what's at risk. Even if the stakes are emotional—losing someone's trust, being forced to face the past—they need to be clear. Ask ChatGPT, "What's an emotional stake I can tie to this scene?" and you'll find ways to make even the quietest moments feel like they matter. That emotional urgency is what turns pages.

Don't forget physical tension, either. Even if there's no big fight or car chase, you can still bring in moments of physical unease. A creaking door. A hand trembling on a coffee cup. A character too still, too quiet. Ask ChatGPT, "Add physical tension to this scene to suggest something is off," and you'll get cues that layer mood and unease right into the action.

Finally, remember that unresolved conflict isn't a mistake—it's a strategy. Not everything needs to be solved right away. In fact, keeping some conflict unresolved across multiple chapters can become the throughline that holds your novel together. Whether it's a long-burning rivalry, a romantic tension, or a mystery that unfolds piece by piece, ChatGPT can help you track and escalate it. Ask, "How can I increase the emotional tension between these two characters in small ways across five chapters?" and you'll get a mini blueprint for rising conflict that pays off big later.

Tension is what keeps your story alive, and when you make it a habit—when you bake it into *every* chapter—it becomes part of the pulse of your book. With ChatGPT as your partner, you don't have to wonder if the scene is too quiet, too slow, or too neat. Just ask how to make it sting a little more, pull a little harder, or leave just enough undone that the reader has to turn the page. Because that's what tension does—it hooks us, grips us, and never lets go.

Writing Emotional Beats That Resonate

When readers talk about the stories that changed them, they're not just remembering the plot. They're remembering how it *felt*. The ache of a goodbye. The rush of a first kiss. The cold shock of betrayal. These are emotional beats—those moments in the story that hit straight in the heart and stay there. If your book has emotional beats that land, it doesn't matter if you wrote it in a month or a single day. The reader won't care how long it took. They'll care that it moved them. And with ChatGPT as your co-writer, you can tap into these emotional moments quickly, effectively, and truthfully—even when you're racing the clock.

Emotional beats are not just about dramatic scenes. They can be tiny, quiet, even wordless. A glance. A hesitation. A character choosing *not* to say something. These moments matter because they reveal truth—about who someone is, what they feel, and what they're afraid to admit. When you write with emotional honesty, the scene doesn't just tell the reader what's happening—it makes them *feel* it. And that's the kind of writing that resonates.

The first step is knowing what your character is feeling—even if they don't know it themselves. Ask ChatGPT, "What is my protagonist actually feeling in this scene even if they won't say it out loud?" and you'll get emotional undercurrents you can write toward. If your character is lashing out, maybe they're scared. If they're cracking jokes, maybe they're deflecting grief. The real emotional beat is never on the surface. It's what's *underneath* that gives a scene depth.

Every major emotional moment should answer—or challenge—one of the character's internal needs. Love, approval, safety, freedom, belonging. When something threatens or fulfills one of those needs, the emotional response becomes powerful. You can tell ChatGPT, "Write an emotional beat where the protagonist feels seen for the first time," and it'll give you the bones of a scene that taps into that deep human longing. You can use that structure and rewrite it in your character's unique voice.

The best emotional beats often come in the *silences*. When the character almost says something but doesn't. When they pause too long. When they walk away instead of staying. Ask ChatGPT, "Write a scene where two characters say very little but communicate a huge emotional shift," and you'll get lines of dialogue and physical cues that say everything without needing to spell it out. Because sometimes, what's *not* said is louder than what is.

Another key to emotional resonance is vulnerability. Readers connect with characters when they're exposed—when they drop the mask. But the timing matters. It has to be earned. A character who's been holding it together finally breaking down carries way more weight than someone who cries in every chapter. Ask ChatGPT, "What would be a powerful moment for this character to break emotionally?" and you'll get suggestions that match the arc and make the emotional beat feel honest, not forced.

Pacing plays a big role too. If everything happens too fast, the reader won't have time to feel it. Slow down just enough in emotional moments to let them breathe. This doesn't mean long-winded internal monologue. It means giving the character space—literally on the page—to absorb what just happened. Use pauses, simple actions, physical sensations. Ask ChatGPT, "How can I slow down this emotional beat without losing momentum?" and it'll give you tricks to hold tension while letting emotion rise.

Sensory detail is your friend here. Emotional beats resonate when they're grounded in the body. A racing heart, trembling fingers, a taste in the mouth, a scent from a memory—these details trigger the reader's own emotional memory. Ask ChatGPT, "Give me physical descriptions that reflect rising panic or quiet heartbreak," and use them not to tell, but to evoke. The goal is for the reader to *feel alongside* your character, not just observe them.

You can also use setting to amplify emotional beats. A goodbye in the rain. A realization at sunset. A confession in a dim hallway. The setting can mirror the feeling, or contrast it to create emotional complexity. Ask ChatGPT, "What kind of setting would heighten the emotional impact of a character letting go of the past?" and you'll get visuals that enhance the mood and deepen the resonance.

Conflict sharpens emotion. If everything's going smoothly, emotional beats don't land as hard. There needs to be tension—even in a love scene. Especially in a love scene. The push-pull, the hesitation, the risk of rejection or misunderstanding—that's where the emotional power lives. You can say to ChatGPT, "Make this romantic beat more emotionally charged with internal conflict," and you'll get dialogue, gestures, and thoughts that elevate it from sweet to unforgettable.

One of the most powerful kinds of emotional beat is the *unexpected* one. When a character reacts in a way they—and the reader—don't see coming. A villain showing mercy. A stoic parent crying. A character forgiving someone they said they never could. Ask ChatGPT, "What's a surprising but true emotional reaction this character could have in this scene?" and let it help you explore new emotional angles. These surprises ring true when they're grounded in what's already been planted—and they stick with readers long after the chapter ends.

Don't be afraid to repeat emotional motifs. A single action—like a hand on a shoulder, a whispered word, a favorite song—can show up multiple times with different meanings. The first time it might be comforting. The next time, devastating. These repeated emotional symbols create resonance because they change as the character changes. Ask ChatGPT, "What small recurring detail could reflect this character's emotional journey?" and you'll get ideas that layer your story with emotional echoes.

And remember: not every emotional beat has to be devastating. Joy, awe, relief, pride—these moments can be just as resonant. What matters is that the emotion feels earned. Ask ChatGPT, "Write a quiet moment of triumph that feels deeply personal," and you'll get a beat that doesn't shout but sings. Often, it's those quiet emotional wins that hit the hardest.

At the end of your writing sprint, it's the emotional beats that will make your book linger in someone's mind. They won't remember every twist or line of dialogue, but they'll remember how it made them *feel*. And with ChatGPT helping you dig deeper, slow down, and write with truth, you'll be surprised how quickly those moments come together—even when you're working fast.

So pause before each key scene. Ask: what is the emotional core of this moment? Then let ChatGPT help you uncover it, express it, and elevate it—until the reader isn't just watching the story unfold, but living it with your characters, heart to heart.

ChatGPT and the Hero's Journey

The Hero's Journey is one of the most powerful story structures in fiction, and for good reason—it taps into deep, universal rhythms of transformation that resonate across cultures and time periods. It's the path of growth, the arc of leaving behind the familiar, facing trials, and returning changed. Whether you're writing a fantasy epic, a romantic drama, a sci-fi thriller, or even a quiet character study, the Hero's Journey can shape your story into something timeless and emotionally satisfying. And when you're writing an entire book in one day, ChatGPT becomes the ultimate shortcut to guiding your character through that mythic structure, step by step, without the heavy lifting.

The Hero's Journey is usually broken down into stages: the ordinary world, the call to adventure, refusal of the call, meeting the mentor, crossing the threshold, trials and allies and enemies, the innermost cave, the ordeal, the reward, the road back, resurrection, and return with the elixir. But you don't have to follow this map rigidly. It's a compass, not a cage. The important part is that your protagonist starts in one place—mentally, emotionally, spiritually—and ends somewhere else, transformed. And ChatGPT can help you build that transformation fast.

Start by defining the ordinary world. What does your hero's life look like before everything changes? It doesn't have to be dramatic. Maybe they're stuck in a routine, ignoring a dream, numbing out from trauma, or hiding from the truth. Ask ChatGPT, "Describe a protagonist's ordinary world that they need to escape from," and you'll get a setting, mood, and emotional status quo that sets the stage for change.

Next comes the call to adventure. Something interrupts that ordinary world—a message, a crisis, a question, a discovery. It's the moment the plot kicks in. You can ask ChatGPT, "What's a compelling inciting incident for a character who's afraid to face their past?" and you'll get story beats that launch your character out of their comfort zone and into the unknown.

Then comes the refusal of the call—because let's be honest, most of us don't leap into change. We resist. So should your character. They might deny, delay, or try to bargain. ChatGPT can help here too: "Write a scene where the hero tries to avoid the adventure, but life won't let them." This moment makes the decision to go forward feel earned, not accidental.

Meeting the mentor is a classic moment in the Hero's Journey. It could be a literal mentor—a wise figure, a guide, a friend—or something symbolic, like a journal left behind, a dream, or a memory. Ask ChatGPT, "Who or what could serve as an unexpected mentor figure for this hero?" and you'll get unique, creative ideas that steer your character in the right direction without making it feel cliché.

Crossing the threshold is the point of no return. The hero leaves the ordinary world behind and steps into the new. This might be physical—a border, a doorway, a journey—or emotional. It marks a shift in tone and stakes. You can say, "Help me write a scene where the protagonist crosses into the unknown, both literally and emotionally," and ChatGPT will give you a launching point for the real adventure.

Now come the tests, allies, and enemies. This is where your story can have fun. Challenges, misunderstandings, conflicts, friendships—this section builds momentum. Ask ChatGPT, "What are three trials my protagonist can face that will challenge their belief system?" and you'll get mini arcs that develop character while keeping the plot moving.

The innermost cave is where your character faces their deepest fear or biggest internal truth. It's quiet. It's intense. It might not even involve external action—it could be a conversation, a memory, a moment of doubt. Ask ChatGPT,

"What would force my protagonist to confront the truth they've been avoiding?" and you'll get a powerful emotional turning point that sets up the climax.

Then comes the ordeal—the climax, the big confrontation, the test that determines who they've become. This could be a fight, a loss, a decision. It's where everything's on the line. You can prompt, "Give me a climactic moment where the protagonist must choose between what they want and what's right," and ChatGPT will help you shape a high-stakes, emotionally charged scene.

After the ordeal, there's the reward—the insight, the growth, the relationship, the knowledge. Maybe the hero gets what they wanted, or maybe they lose it but find something better. You can say, "What's an emotionally satisfying reward for a character who's spent the story hiding from vulnerability?" and you'll get a meaningful resolution that aligns with the journey.

Then it's time for the road back. The character begins their return, but things aren't the same. Sometimes there's a final twist, or a last challenge that tests everything they've learned. ChatGPT can help you write this pivot: "Add a final moment of doubt before the hero fully claims their growth."

The resurrection is the final test—the rebirth. It's where the hero applies everything they've learned, usually under pressure. This is their transformation moment. It could be quiet or explosive. Ask ChatGPT, "What would a resurrection scene look like for a hero who finally accepts their self-worth?" and you'll get a rich, resonant beat that shows the full arc of their growth.

And finally, the return with the elixir. The hero comes back changed, and they bring something valuable with them—wisdom, peace, love, truth, hope. It's not just about the hero. It's about what they give back to the world. Ask ChatGPT, "How can I write a final scene that shows the hero's growth affecting others?" and you'll close your story in a way that feels whole.

Using the Hero's Journey doesn't mean locking yourself into a formula. It means having a reliable map to follow—and a way to make your character arc resonate with universal emotional truths. With ChatGPT, you don't have to reinvent the wheel or get lost in the weeds. You just pick your moments, prompt with purpose, and let the structure guide you as you write.

So the next time you're stuck on where to go next, or how to deepen a character's arc, or how to raise the stakes, remember the Hero's Journey is right there—and ChatGPT can walk the path with you, step by step, scene by scene, from the call to adventure to the final return. And best of all? You can do it all in a day.

Using ChatGPT for Theme Exploration and Consistency

Theme is what gives your story its emotional backbone. It's the underlying message, question, or idea that weaves through every scene, quietly shaping the narrative from the shadows. It's not the plot. It's not the character arc. It's what those things are *about*. And when your theme is clear, consistent, and thoughtfully explored, readers come away feeling like they experienced something bigger than just events on a page. Writing a whole fiction book in one day might sound like you have no time to think about theme—but with ChatGPT helping you, you can identify, develop, and reinforce a powerful theme as you go, without missing a beat.

Let's start with discovery. Sometimes you already know your theme before you write. Sometimes it reveals itself during the process. Either way, ChatGPT can help you clarify what your story is really saying beneath the surface. Try asking, "Based on this plot summary, what themes seem to be emerging?" You might get responses like redemption, identity, freedom vs. control, love vs. fear, or the cost of ambition. Once you see what themes are embedded in your story, you can make a conscious choice: lean in, expand, and reinforce.

Themes don't have to be complicated. In fact, the best ones often aren't. A theme can be as simple as "Everyone deserves a second chance" or "You can't run from who you are." The key is to let that idea resonate—not by spelling it out, but by letting it echo in the choices characters make, the outcomes of conflicts, the questions that never get answered. Once you land on your core theme, you can ask ChatGPT, "How can I reinforce the theme of self-acceptance through subplots and dialogue?" and it'll give you subtle ways to work it in across the story.

One of the best ways to express theme is through character conflict. When characters believe different things about the world—about love, about justice, about power—their clashes naturally reveal what the story is *about*. Ask ChatGPT, "What opposing beliefs could create conflict between two characters in a story about forgiveness?" and you'll get character dynamics that double as theme exploration. These philosophical differences create tension *and* depth.

You can also explore theme through symbolism and recurring motifs. Maybe the theme is about control, and you use broken watches, locked doors, and cages as recurring imagery. Or maybe it's about freedom, and birds, open skies, and wind keep showing up. These little touches don't shout the theme—they whisper it. Ask ChatGPT, "What symbolic objects or recurring elements could reflect a theme of grief and healing?" and you'll get a toolkit of subtle details to pepper throughout your scenes.

Dialogue is another great place to explore theme—especially when characters talk around it, challenge it, or unknowingly reflect it. A line like "Some people just don't change" means more when the theme is transformation. Or a throwaway line like "It's better to feel nothing than to get hurt again" hits harder when your protagonist is on a journey toward vulnerability. You can use ChatGPT to find these thematic echoes. Try, "Write a conversation between two characters where one expresses doubt and the other reveals hope, aligned with a theme of resilience," and you'll get dialogue that feels authentic and on-message.

To keep your theme consistent without being repetitive, try viewing each major plot beat through a thematic lens. For every big moment, ask: what does this say about the theme? How does it support or challenge the message I'm exploring? You can even run your scene summary through ChatGPT and ask, "How does this scene reflect or contradict the theme of identity?" This helps you avoid scenes that feel disconnected or random, and keeps the emotional thread strong all the way through.

Subplots are another great tool for reinforcing theme. Your secondary characters don't need to repeat the protagonist's journey—but their stories can reflect, contrast, or complicate the core theme. If your main story is about truth, maybe a subplot explores lies of omission. If the theme is justice, maybe a side character chooses revenge instead of fairness. Ask ChatGPT, "What subplot could reflect the theme of sacrifice from a different angle?" and use that contrast to add dimension and richness.

Even your setting and atmosphere can carry the theme. A crumbling city might reflect decay and rebirth. A winter landscape can echo emotional isolation. A chaotic market might reflect inner conflict. These elements don't need to be heavy-handed. They just need to gently support the emotional tone of the story. Ask ChatGPT, "What kind of setting would subtly reinforce a theme of rebirth?" and you'll get worldbuilding that feels intentional and thematically aligned.

If you're unsure whether your theme is coming through clearly, use ChatGPT as a story reader. Say, "Based on this chapter, what themes are coming across to you?" and it will tell you what a reader might pick up subconsciously. If it's not aligned with what you intended, you can go back and nudge the scenes into better focus. If it *is* aligned, you've got confirmation that the theme is landing.

Another way to keep your theme consistent is by defining a list of emotional or thematic touchstones for your story. Words like freedom, loss, hope, guilt, family. Keep them visible while you write. Then, if you ever get stuck or your writing starts to feel flat, ask ChatGPT, "How can I bring the theme of freedom back into this moment?" and you'll get ideas that reconnect you to your story's soul.

You can even plan your whole story with theme at the center. Give ChatGPT your theme and ask, "What kind of character arc would best explore this idea?" or "What kind of plot naturally tests a character's belief in this theme?" Now you're not just writing a story with a theme—you're writing a story *about* that theme. That's where emotional resonance lives.

Theme doesn't mean hitting your reader over the head with a message. It means crafting a world where ideas live beneath the surface, where choices matter, where symbols linger, and where the emotional truth rises slowly until the reader feels it in their bones. With ChatGPT guiding your prompts, nudging your scenes, and helping you connect the dots, you don't have to choose between speed and depth. You can write fast *and* write meaningfully.

So don't wait until the end to think about theme. Start early. Plant it everywhere. Water it in dialogue, nurture it in conflict, and harvest it in your ending. Ask questions. Push back. Dig deeper. And let ChatGPT help you shape a story where every line, every scene, and every choice hums with something bigger underneath. Because when a story has a heart—and that heart beats in rhythm with a powerful theme—it resonates long after the final word.

How to Handle Flashbacks and Time Jumps with Style

Flashbacks and time jumps can be some of the most effective storytelling tools in your writer's toolbox—but only if they're handled with care. Used well, they add depth, context, and emotional power to your story. They let readers understand where a character's been, what shaped them, and why the present matters so much. But if you fumble the transition or overload your story with clunky flashbacks, you risk confusing your reader, disrupting the flow, or even dragging down your pacing. When you're writing a full book in one day with ChatGPT, managing flashbacks and time shifts with clarity and elegance becomes a game-changer. The good news is that the right prompt at the right moment can make these tricky elements feel seamless and cinematic.

Let's start with why you might use a flashback. It's not just about filling in backstory—it's about *emotional context*. A character's decision in the present becomes more powerful when we understand the pain, joy, or trauma behind it. A flashback should do more than explain. It should *reveal*. Ask ChatGPT, "What moment from the past could make this decision more emotionally charged?" and you'll get potential flashback scenes that feel urgent, not indulgent. When the past collides with the present, you get resonance—and that's when flashbacks shine.

The timing of your flashbacks matters just as much as their content. Drop one too early, and it risks slowing the forward momentum. Drop it too late, and the reader might not care anymore. A well-placed flashback should either raise the emotional stakes of a scene or answer a burning question that's been building. Try asking ChatGPT, "Where's the best point in the story to reveal this key past event for maximum emotional impact?" and you'll get suggestions that align with your pacing and character arc.

Transitioning into a flashback should feel smooth, not like the story is hitting a speed bump. One trick is to use a sensory trigger—something in the present that reminds the character of the past. A sound, a smell, a phrase, a photograph. You can prompt ChatGPT with, "Write a seamless transition from present action into a memory triggered by a smell," and it will give you natural ways to lead into a flashback without jarring the reader. These kinds of transitions help the flashback feel like a continuation of the emotional thread, rather than a hard detour.

You also need to signal clearly to the reader that a time shift is happening. This doesn't mean writing "Ten years earlier" in bold font—though that works for some stories. It can be as simple as a change in verb tense, a shift in tone, or a clear emotional marker that the character is drifting into memory. Ask ChatGPT, "How can I cue a flashback without breaking the narrative flow?" and it'll offer language techniques to guide the reader smoothly and keep them grounded.

Once you're in the flashback, keep it focused. A flashback isn't an info dump. It's a scene. It has tension, stakes, emotion. Don't just tell us what happened—*show* us. Let the reader live through it with the character. You can even use ChatGPT to help keep the flashback tight and punchy: "Rewrite this flashback to increase emotional tension and trim unnecessary exposition." You'll get a sharper version that still delivers the emotional payload without overstaying its welcome.

When the flashback ends, how you return to the present matters just as much. The character should emerge from the memory changed—or at least more aware. The flashback should ripple forward into their next action or decision. Ask ChatGPT, "Write a transition from the end of a flashback back into present action, showing how the memory affects the character's state of mind," and you'll get more than just a fade-in—you'll get narrative momentum.

Time jumps—meaning bigger shifts forward or backward across the timeline—should be handled with even more care. These aren't just memory scenes. They can represent new acts, new phases in character development, or even plot pivots. To keep them stylish and clear, you need to give the reader something to hold onto. That could be an image, a theme, a phrase that repeats in both time periods. You can ask ChatGPT, "What's a symbolic thread I can use to connect this past chapter to a present chapter across a time jump?" and you'll get a recurring motif that smooths the leap and makes it feel intentional.

Flashbacks don't always need to be chapters. Sometimes they work beautifully in small doses—a line, a paragraph, a brief moment of recollection that flashes and fades. These micro-flashbacks can be used for emotional layering without derailing the scene. Try prompting, "Give me a two-line memory that interrupts a tense moment with emotional weight," and you'll get a short burst of backstory that hits hard and then disappears, leaving its emotional residue behind.

In stories that are nonlinear by design—where the timeline jumps around a lot—consistency and clarity become even more important. If you're writing this kind of narrative, ChatGPT can help you structure it cleanly: "Give me a chapter layout for a nonlinear story exploring memory, guilt, and redemption." You'll get a roadmap that makes sure each time shift has a purpose and a place.

Another stylish approach is using dual timelines that unfold in parallel. These can create suspense, thematic resonance, or reveal connections across generations. You can ask ChatGPT, "How can I use a dual-timeline structure to gradually reveal a family secret?" and it'll help you plot out which events to show when, and how the timelines can echo or contrast each other.

The key to using flashbacks and time jumps well is *control*. You're not just jumping around for fun—you're revealing story in a way that deepens meaning and emotion. If a memory doesn't reveal character or push the plot, it probably doesn't belong. But when used with intent and precision, flashbacks can transform a flat narrative into something rich, emotional, and layered.

ChatGPT is especially useful when you're short on time and need to make quick decisions. Should this memory be a full scene or a passing thought? Should this reveal come now or later? Ask the AI. Test ideas. Rewrite transitions. Find the best emotional entry and exit points. You don't need to spend hours restructuring or second-guessing—you can move quickly and still write with confidence.

So if your story wants to jump through time, let it. Just do it with style. Treat each shift as a moment of purpose. Tie the past to the present, and let the emotional truths echo between them. With ChatGPT by your side, every flashback can land with clarity and power—and every time jump can feel like part of the plan, not just a detour.

Weaving Subplots without Losing Focus

Subplots are where a story breathes. They give your characters dimension, your world texture, and your themes extra depth. A well-woven subplot can mirror the main story, challenge the protagonist, reveal hidden layers, or build relationships that make the climax hit even harder. But let's be honest—when you're writing a whole book in one day, subplots can feel like dangerous territory. Add too many, and suddenly your story gets bloated. Add the wrong one, and it feels like a distraction. The trick is weaving them in with care, so they enhance the main plot without stealing the spotlight. And that's exactly where ChatGPT becomes your best ally.

A subplot, at its core, is a story within your story. It has its own mini arc—beginning, middle, and end. But instead of competing with your main plot, it supports it. It might be about a supporting character's growth. It might explore a theme from another angle. It might add emotional weight, comic relief, romantic tension, or philosophical complexity. The secret is to build subplots that are *relevant*. You want them to echo, contrast, or challenge the journey your protagonist is already on.

Start by identifying what your main story is really about. What is your protagonist struggling with? What's the core emotional journey? Once you've got that, ask ChatGPT: "What subplot would challenge or reflect a main plot about self-forgiveness?" You'll get suggestions that are thematically aligned—like a character refusing to forgive someone else, or a parallel arc about letting go of guilt. These connections are what keep the subplot from feeling like filler.

One of the easiest ways to weave in a subplot without losing focus is to link it directly to a supporting character who's already part of the main story. Maybe it's your protagonist's best friend chasing a personal dream. Maybe it's a love interest facing a moral dilemma. The subplot doesn't need its own cast and setting—it can live inside the existing structure. Ask ChatGPT, "How can I build a subplot around the protagonist's sister that intersects with the main storyline?" and you'll get layered, character-driven ideas that naturally tie into what's already happening.

Timing matters, too. You don't want to introduce all your subplots at once. Let them emerge as the main story develops. When the plot slows or needs a moment of reflection, that's a great time to dip into a subplot. Think of it like breathing room—not a detour, but a deepening. You can ask ChatGPT, "Where in my outline is the best place to introduce a subplot without disrupting the main momentum?" and it will help you find the perfect pocket to expand your story without derailing it.

To keep subplots tight and purposeful, make sure they do one of three things: raise the stakes, explore the theme, or develop character. If a subplot doesn't do at least one of those, it's probably not necessary. When in doubt, run it through ChatGPT: "Does this subplot about a romantic interest raise the stakes or reveal something new about the protagonist?" You'll get feedback that helps you decide whether to keep it, cut it, or reshape it.

Subplots can also serve as mirrors or contrasts to the main plot. If your protagonist is learning to trust, maybe a subplot shows another character's betrayal. If your main arc is about survival, maybe the subplot deals with sacrifice. These thematic connections give your story cohesion. Ask ChatGPT, "What subplot would thematically contrast a main plot about ambition and obsession?" and you'll get angles that add tension and complexity without confusing the focus.

Another benefit of subplots is pacing control. When the main story is too intense for too long, cutting to a subplot gives readers a breather. And when the subplot builds tension on its own, it can keep momentum going while the main plot resets. Think of your story like a weave—main plot and subplot threading in and out, keeping the texture interesting.

Ask ChatGPT, "How can I alternate scenes between the main story and a subplot without confusing the reader?" and you'll get structural tips to keep everything flowing smoothly.

Subplots are also a great place for character relationships to grow. Whether it's romance, friendship, rivalry, or mentorship, giving those dynamics their own little story arc can make the emotional payoff of your climax much stronger. For example, a subplot about a strained friendship that slowly rebuilds might climax when the friend makes a key choice during the final conflict. You can ask ChatGPT, "Outline a short subplot that deepens a friendship while reinforcing the theme of redemption," and you'll get something tightly focused and emotionally rich.

Keep an eye on how you resolve your subplots. Don't leave them dangling—or worse, resolve them too early and then ignore them. The best subplots either converge with the main plot at the climax or resolve just before it, contributing to the emotional or narrative weight of the final act. Ask ChatGPT, "How should this subplot resolve so it supports the main climax?" and you'll get suggestions that tie it all together without stealing the thunder from your central arc.

Also, don't forget that not all subplots need equal screen time. Some are quick beats that return only once or twice, while others grow alongside the main story. The key is balance. You can ask ChatGPT, "Which subplot should get the most focus in a 10-chapter novel about grief and healing?" and get guidance on how to prioritize what matters most.

Finally, let your subplots evolve naturally. You don't need to plan every twist. Let the characters react to events in the main plot, and the subplot will grow. If you're unsure where it's headed, ask ChatGPT mid-draft, "What's a surprising but fitting turn for this subplot at this point in the story?" You might find that what started as background ends up becoming emotionally essential.

Subplots, when used well, don't slow your story down—they *lift* it. They add shadows, contrast, nuance, and texture. They make your characters feel real, your world feel lived-in, and your themes feel deeper. And with ChatGPT helping you brainstorm, refine, and interweave those threads, you can stay focused on your main arc without sacrificing richness. You don't have to choose between tight plotting and layered storytelling. You just have to keep everything connected.

So don't be afraid of subplots, even on a one-day deadline. Invite them in. Give them purpose. Let them reflect, support, or challenge your central story. And most of all, let them resonate—quietly, powerfully—just beneath the surface. That's how you write a book that doesn't just move... it echoes.

Planting Setups and Delivering Payoffs

There's a particular kind of satisfaction that comes from reading a story where everything feels intentional—where the smallest moment in chapter one suddenly explodes with meaning in chapter twenty. That's the magic of setups and payoffs. When done right, they create a sense of cohesion and narrative intelligence that makes your reader trust you completely. They'll keep turning pages because they believe everything matters—and when the payoff lands, it feels earned. And here's the good news: even when you're writing an entire novel in a single day, you can still craft elegant setups and satisfying payoffs with the help of ChatGPT.

A setup is anything you introduce that suggests future importance. It can be a line of dialogue, a character trait, an object, a relationship, a belief, a fear, or even a casual moment that sticks out just enough to raise a tiny question in the reader's mind. The payoff is when that element returns—often in a surprising but inevitable way—to deliver emotional, thematic, or narrative impact. Think of it as planting a seed early and watching it bloom just when the story needs it most.

The trick is to know what you're planting. Even if you're writing fast, you can still be intentional. Once you have your basic outline, take a few minutes and ask ChatGPT, "What elements from the first act could return later in the story as payoffs?" You'll get a list of moments that can be echoed, reversed, or expanded upon later in the book. These become your invisible threads—tiny clues that tie the story together.

Let's say your protagonist picks up a strange coin in chapter one. Maybe it seems like just a quirky detail. But if that coin is used in the final chapter to unlock a secret door, now it's a payoff. The reader remembers it, feels the click, and trusts you more. You can ask ChatGPT, "What are subtle ways to reintroduce a small object from early in the story to make it meaningful later?" and it'll help you connect the dots without making it too obvious.

Not all payoffs have to be plot-driven. Emotional payoffs are just as powerful. A character who's afraid of water because of a past trauma might finally dive in to save someone they care about. That's a payoff of a fear that was planted early. Ask ChatGPT, "How can I structure an emotional arc with a setup and payoff around this character's fear of failure?" and you'll get a road map for turning a personal struggle into a triumphant resolution.

Themes can also be set up and paid off. If your story begins with a character saying, "Some people never change," and ends with that same character learning that people *do* change—especially themselves—that's a thematic payoff. It hits harder because the idea has been there, growing quietly under the surface. You can prompt ChatGPT with, "What are examples of theme-driven dialogue that can be mirrored later for emotional impact?" and it'll give you lines that grow in meaning as the story unfolds.

Another fun technique is reversal. You set something up, then twist it. A weapon that once saved the protagonist becomes a danger. A trusted friend becomes a traitor. A character's greatest strength becomes their weakness. ChatGPT can help you brainstorm these twists on the fly: "What's a setup I can invert later in the story for dramatic effect?" This gives your narrative a feeling of evolution—nothing is static, and everything changes meaning over time.

Pacing is key when it comes to setups and payoffs. If the gap between the two is too short, it can feel unearned. Too long, and the reader might forget the setup. But there are ways to keep setups alive subtly—by reminding the reader through repetition or emotional echoes. You can ask ChatGPT, "How can I remind readers about an early setup without making it too obvious?" and you'll get tips for reinforcing the element through character thoughts, offhand comments, or recurring imagery.

You can also write backwards. Start with the payoff you want—the big reveal, the final decision, the moment of truth—and ask, "What would I need to plant earlier in the story to make this moment feel earned?" ChatGPT is great at reverse-engineering your climax. Say, "Here's the final scene. What are three things I need to foreshadow to make this land emotionally and logically?" That way, even when you're working fast, your story still has that layered, thoughtful feel.

In a one-day writing sprint, it's tempting to focus only on what's happening now. But if you take just a few seconds at the end of each chapter to ask ChatGPT, "Is there anything I've set up that I should revisit later?" you'll be able to track your story's promises—and keep them. You're building trust with your reader, scene by scene.

Another great trick is the *callback*. It doesn't have to be huge. A line of dialogue repeated in a new context. A joke that gets turned serious. A lesson ignored the first time that finally gets learned. These call-backs feel like echoes through the story, and they're deeply satisfying. Ask ChatGPT, "Suggest a callback for this line in chapter 2 that would have emotional impact in the final chapter," and you'll get ideas that transform simple moments into meaningful ones.

Don't forget that even small moments can be payoffs. A character finally saying "I'm sorry." Someone choosing kindness instead of revenge. A side character returning when least expected. These quiet beats are often the ones that stick. With ChatGPT, you can explore small setups that build into something beautiful. Try, "Give me a small gesture in chapter 1 that could come full circle in chapter 10," and you'll find ways to layer your story with richness.

Ultimately, setups and payoffs are about *intentionality*. They say to the reader, "I've thought this through. Every moment counts." And when done well, they make your story feel tighter, smarter, and more emotionally resonant. With ChatGPT, you don't have to keep everything in your head or map it all out in advance. You just need to ask the right questions, recognize opportunities, and let your story echo and build on itself as you go.

So as you write, keep your eyes open for those little details, throwaway lines, and early choices. Ask yourself, "Could this come back later?" Ask ChatGPT how. And when the time is right, drop the payoff—not with a shout, but with that quiet click of narrative destiny. That's how you write a story that sticks with people. One setup, one payoff, one satisfying moment at a time.

Writing a Gripping Opening Scene

The first scene of your novel is everything. It's the handshake, the promise, the hook—and if it's not gripping, readers won't stick around long enough to see the brilliance waiting on page two. In a one-day writing sprint, the temptation might be to rush past the opening just to get moving. But a great beginning sets the tone, pace, and emotional core of your entire story. The good news? With ChatGPT by your side, you can build an opening scene that hooks hard, introduces key elements smoothly, and leaves readers leaning forward, hungry for more.

A gripping opening doesn't need explosions or action—though it can have them. What it *needs* is tension, intrigue, and something unresolved. You're not giving away everything in the first few paragraphs, but you are inviting the reader into a world where something is happening—or about to happen. Ask ChatGPT, "Give me an opening scene idea that starts in the middle of tension without requiring a lot of setup," and you'll get a list of compelling moments: a character running from something unseen, a whispered conversation interrupted, a deal going wrong, or a quiet moment before a storm breaks.

The trick to a powerful opening is dropping the reader straight into *motion*. Not necessarily literal movement, but narrative momentum. A character making a choice. A situation unraveling. A line of dialogue that leaves a question hanging. You can try a prompt like, "Write an opening paragraph where the protagonist is already in the middle of something going wrong," and ChatGPT will help you get past the dreaded 'blank page' by generating a strong entry point.

It's also important to introduce a sense of character right away. Readers don't need the full backstory in the first chapter—but they do need someone to *care about*. That might mean someone flawed, someone struggling, someone funny, or someone mysterious. Ask ChatGPT, "How can I show my protagonist's core emotional struggle in the first scene without exposition?" and you'll get moments of behavior, dialogue, or internal reaction that reveal character without info-dumping.

Your setting matters, too. It doesn't have to be described in paragraphs of detail, but a few sharp, well-chosen elements can anchor the reader in the world and establish tone. Ask ChatGPT, "Give me atmospheric details for a tense opening scene set in a crumbling seaside town," and you'll get visual, auditory, and tactile cues that set a vivid mood instantly. Think of it like a snapshot—a frame that tells us something essential about the world we're entering.

Another trick is to open with a question—not a literal one, but a narrative one. Something that makes the reader ask: Why is this happening? What are they running from? What happens next? You can use ChatGPT to test this directly: "Does this scene create enough intrigue to make the reader curious about what's coming?" or "How can I revise this paragraph to raise a compelling story question?" The goal is to plant a seed of curiosity that can't be ignored.

Dialogue can be a powerful opener, especially when it's surprising, emotional, or contains subtext. A line like, "You really think they won't find the body?" immediately raises stakes and questions. Or something quiet but strange like, "That's the third time the moon's changed color this week." Ask ChatGPT, "Write an opening exchange between two characters that hints at a mystery," and you'll get banter or conflict that immediately pulls the reader in.

Starting with a character's emotional state is another effective entry point. Show them scared, furious, heartbroken, euphoric—but do it in motion. A woman crying alone doesn't hook as hard as a woman calmly smiling while burying a wedding ring. Ask ChatGPT, "Write a first scene where the protagonist is feeling something intense but trying to hide it," and you'll get a dynamic emotional beat layered with tension and subtext.

If you want a more atmospheric or lyrical opening, go for tone—but keep it tethered to something happening. You can open with a storm building over a city, but we need to know *why* that matters, even if the reason is only hinted at. Ask ChatGPT, "Give me a moody opening that sets the tone for a psychological thriller," and you'll get sensory cues and pacing that build unease while setting the stage for the story to come.

One common mistake with openings is to overload them with backstory or explanation. The first scene should be *experienced*, not narrated. We don't need to know everything yet—just enough to care. You can feed your draft into ChatGPT and ask, "Which parts of this opening slow the pacing or reveal too much too early?" and get a trimmed version that stays sharp and focused.

A great opening also hints at the theme or emotional arc of the story. If your book is about transformation, show a character trapped in a version of themselves. If it's about justice, open with a moment of injustice. You don't need to hit the reader over the head—just give them a taste. Ask ChatGPT, "Suggest a first scene that introduces the theme of identity vs. conformity," and you'll get a slice of your larger story that fits right into the beginning.

And don't forget the final line of the opening scene. It's just as important as the first. It should push the reader into the next chapter. Maybe it's a twist, a threat, a vow, or just a lingering unease. Ask ChatGPT, "Give me three options for a punchy last line to end this opening chapter," and choose the one that gives your reader a reason to keep reading.

In the end, the goal of a gripping opening scene isn't to show off or overexplain—it's to *hook* emotionally, mentally, and atmospherically. It's to promise the reader that the ride ahead is worth taking. With ChatGPT helping you brainstorm, refine, and focus, you don't have to stumble your way into the story—you can leap in, bold and confident, from line one.

So trust your instincts. Start in motion. Keep it lean. Ask the right questions. And let that first scene crackle with the tension, intrigue, and emotion that only you can bring to the page. Because if you hook the reader from the very beginning, the rest of your one-day novel will already have momentum in its favor.

Midpoint Twists That Reshape the Whole Story

The middle of your novel is a crucial turning point—it's where stories either pick up serious momentum or start to sag. That midpoint moment isn't just a place to "check in." It's an opportunity to completely shake up the world of your story, to reveal something the reader didn't see coming, or to force your protagonist to see things in a way they never have before. When you're writing a book in a single day, that midpoint twist becomes your best friend—it refuels your narrative, tightens your pacing, and catapults your characters into the second half with purpose and urgency. And the best part? You don't have to wait for inspiration to strike. You can build a midpoint twist on command with a few well-aimed prompts to ChatGPT.

A good midpoint twist does two things at once. First, it reveals new information that changes the way the protagonist—and the reader—understands the story so far. Second, it launches a shift in motivation, goal, or emotional stakes that drives the second half of the book. This is the moment where what the protagonist *thought* they wanted might no longer be enough. Or where the path they were following turns out to lead somewhere entirely unexpected.

Start by thinking about what your character believes to be true at the beginning of the story. What assumptions are they acting on? What goal are they chasing? Then flip the table. You can ask ChatGPT, "What's a revelation that would force my protagonist to question everything they've believed so far?" and you'll get twists that hit deep. Maybe their ally has been working against them. Maybe the villain is someone they've already trusted. Maybe the person they're trying to save doesn't want to be saved.

A great midpoint twist doesn't have to be loud. It doesn't need to be a betrayal or a death or a big dramatic explosion—though it *can* be any of those things. Sometimes, the most powerful midpoint shift is internal. A realization. A loss of innocence. A sudden burst of doubt. Something that reorients the character's sense of self, the stakes, or the rules of the world. You can say to ChatGPT, "Give me a subtle but powerful internal twist for a character who's always been emotionally guarded," and it'll generate ideas that feel true to your story while opening new pathways forward.

In genre fiction, especially mystery, thriller, and fantasy, midpoint twists are also where world-shaking secrets are often revealed. If your story has a mystery element, the midpoint is the perfect time to drop a clue that recontextualizes everything. Ask ChatGPT, "What's a midpoint revelation that makes the protagonist realize they've been chasing the wrong villain?" and watch the story spin in a new direction—tightening tension and re-energizing the narrative.

Another effective type of midpoint twist is a reversal of power. Maybe the protagonist gains leverage. Maybe they lose it. Maybe someone who seemed insignificant suddenly holds all the cards. You can prompt ChatGPT with, "Show me a scene where the protagonist thinks they've won, only to realize they've been manipulated," and you'll get a setup that builds hope, then yanks it away. These shifts are emotional gold because they create impact and drive character change.

Themes can also come into play at the midpoint. If your story is about identity, the midpoint might be where the character realizes they've been wearing a mask. If it's about freedom, the midpoint might be where they discover the cost of escape. You can ask ChatGPT, "What midpoint twist would bring my story's core theme into sharper focus?" and you'll get ideas that tie your narrative to its emotional spine, making everything feel tighter and more resonant.

If you're unsure what kind of twist fits your story, give ChatGPT a brief summary of your first half—what's been happening, what the character wants, who's been helping or hurting them—and ask, "What kind of twist at the midpoint would make everything more complicated?" The response will usually involve raising the stakes, flipping allegiances, revealing lies, or shifting the character's goal in a meaningful way.

One powerful twist type is the "enemy becomes ally" or "ally becomes enemy." These create emotional dissonance and challenge the protagonist to re-evaluate not only what's happening, but who they are in relation to it. If your story includes multiple characters with conflicting motives, ask ChatGPT, "How can I turn a trusted ally into a threat at the midpoint in a believable way?" and you'll get twists rooted in character that still feel shocking.

A good twist should echo both forward and backward in your story. That means you can go back and plant subtle clues (or misdirects) in earlier chapters. If you're pressed for time, ask ChatGPT, "What are three small setups I can add earlier in the story to support this twist without giving it away?" and you'll get cues to insert or reinforce without doing a massive rewrite. This is how you make your twist feel earned instead of random.

Don't be afraid to get emotional with your twist, either. Maybe your character's worst fear comes true. Maybe they find the person they've been looking for—only to realize they're the villain. Or maybe they get exactly what they wanted... and it doesn't make them feel the way they thought it would. ChatGPT can help here too: "Give me a midpoint twist that shatters the protagonist emotionally but propels them into action." Now your story has momentum *and* weight.

One way to test your twist is to ask: does this change what the story *means*? If everything could keep going the same way afterward, the twist probably isn't strong enough. A real midpoint twist sends shockwaves. It makes the story bigger, deeper, messier, more urgent. If your draft feels flat, feed it to ChatGPT and say, "How can I add a midpoint twist that raises the stakes and changes the character's trajectory?" and you'll get structural suggestions that do exactly that.

Remember: the midpoint is not just the halfway mark. It's the engine shift. The wake-up call. The punch in the gut. It's the moment that says, "You thought you knew what this story was about? Think again." And with ChatGPT helping you craft that moment—layered, believable, and bold—you'll send your second half soaring with energy and emotional payoff.

So don't settle for just coasting through the middle. Flip something. Break something. Reveal something. Let the twist ripple across every scene that follows. That's how you keep your one-day novel tight, powerful, and completely "unputdownable".

Creating Cliffhangers That Beg for More

A great cliffhanger is a magic trick. It makes the reader flip to the next page before their brain even realizes it. It's the gasp at the end of a scene, the half-whispered secret, the door left ajar, the question that demands an answer. If your story is a train, the cliffhanger is the engine—it pulls everything forward. And when you're writing a novel in a single day, cliffhangers aren't just fun—they're essential. They keep your pacing tight, your scenes connected, and your reader glued to the narrative. With ChatGPT riding shotgun, crafting irresistible cliffhangers becomes a smooth, even addictive, part of your process.

The first thing to understand about cliffhangers is that they don't have to be dramatic explosions or death threats—though those work great, too. A cliffhanger is simply *unresolved tension*. It's a moment that says, "Wait... what happens next?" And you can use that tension at the end of every chapter or scene to hook your reader's curiosity.

There are a few classic types of cliffhangers. One of the most obvious is the **interrupted action**. The character opens the door—and what they see is never described. The villain lunges—but we don't know if they strike. The phone rings—and we cut the scene just as someone picks up. Ask ChatGPT, "Write a scene ending where the protagonist discovers something shocking but we don't see what it is," and you'll get suspenseful beats that beg to be followed up.

Another powerful type is the **sudden revelation**. This is when something previously hidden is brought to light at the last moment—a betrayal, a secret identity, a truth that changes everything. When your reader thought they understood what was going on, a well-placed twist at the end of a chapter can flip the entire table. Ask ChatGPT, "What's a jaw-dropping reveal that could happen at this point in the story?" and it will help you land a scene with a bang instead of a fade.

Then there's the **ticking clock** style cliffhanger. You end a chapter with a looming deadline: someone's coming, the bomb is armed, the truth is moments from being exposed. The tension comes not from *what* will happen, but *when*—and the sense that time is running out. Ask ChatGPT, "How can I end this chapter with a time-based threat that forces urgency into the next scene?" and you'll get a suspenseful setup that lingers.

You can also use **emotional cliffhangers**—these are softer, but equally compelling. Maybe someone is about to confess their feelings. Maybe a character learns something that makes them question everything. Maybe they're standing at a crossroads, and the next chapter will decide which way they turn. Ask ChatGPT, "Suggest an emotional dilemma to end this scene that raises internal tension," and you'll get moments that feel deeply personal and dramatically unresolved.

Questions left hanging are also a great strategy. You don't need to answer every mystery right away. In fact, delaying the answer is what keeps the tension alive. Maybe someone finds a letter they're not supposed to read—but we don't know what's inside. Maybe someone is about to say something critical—but the chapter ends before they do. Ask ChatGPT, "What question can I raise at the end of this chapter that will make the reader desperate to keep reading?" and let it craft a teaser you can pay off later.

The best cliffhangers often combine multiple elements—physical danger, emotional stakes, and a story question. For example, "She stepped forward to tell the truth. Then the lights went out." That's part action, part emotion, part mystery. You can ask ChatGPT, "Give me three ways to end this chapter with a multi-layered cliffhanger," and use those to spice up the end of your scenes with depth and punch.

Even subtle cliffhangers can work beautifully. You don't always need fireworks. A soft, quiet moment that leaves something unresolved can create just as much pull. "He smiled—but it didn't reach his eyes." Or, "She thought she was finally safe. Until she heard the knock." These moments of unease, these shadows cast over the next beat, keep the reader leaning in. You can prompt ChatGPT with, "Write a low-key cliffhanger that leaves the reader with a sense of dread," and you'll get that haunting, literary kind of tension.

It's important to match the tone of your cliffhanger with the tone of your story. If you're writing a thriller, you might end with someone being watched from the shadows. If you're writing a romantic drama, you might end with a text message going unanswered. If your story has mystery, maybe it ends with a clue that contradicts everything the characters thought they knew. Ask ChatGPT, "What's a genre-appropriate cliffhanger that fits the mood of this chapter?" and it'll give you something that blends perfectly with your voice.

And here's the trick most writers miss: you don't have to write a perfect cliffhanger from scratch. You can take a completed scene and *tweak* the final line. Just a sentence or two can transform a quiet ending into a cliffhanger. Feed your ending to ChatGPT and ask, "Can you rewrite the last line to turn it into a cliffhanger?" and you'll get options that reframe the moment with tension, mystery, or forward motion.

If you're writing quickly, it helps to have a rhythm. Think of each chapter as ending on a breath held in the chest. Not a period. A pause. A hinge. When you plan your scenes, ask, "Where's the beat that everything turns? What's the unresolved emotion or unanswered question?" Let that moment *be* your ending. Then move on, fast, knowing your reader will follow.

Cliffhangers also help you structure your one-day novel. They mark the trail behind you and light the way ahead. If you ever feel lost in the middle of your draft, stop and ask ChatGPT, "What kind of cliffhanger can turn this quiet chapter into a page-turner?" and it'll re-energize the scene and point toward your next move. When done well, cliffhangers aren't manipulative—they're magnetic. They create flow. They build tension. They spark questions. And most of all, they make your reader need just *one more page*. Then another. Then another. So don't save your cliffhangers for the big finale. Drop them all the way through. Use them to thread suspense into the smallest moments. Let ChatGPT help you craft each one with variety, precision, and emotional bite. Because when you're writing a novel in a day, you don't want your story to just move forward—you want it to *drag the reader with it*. Cliffhangers are how you make that happen. One page at a time.

Writing a Satisfying Ending That Delivers

A satisfying ending doesn't mean tying every ribbon in a perfect bow—it means giving your reader the emotional payoff they didn't even know they were waiting for. It's the echo of your opening, the full-circle moment, the quiet breath or explosive beat that says, "This is where it all led." After writing a novel in one day, you might feel tempted to coast into the final chapter with a few hasty wrap-ups and a smile. But the ending is what leaves the lasting impression. It's the feeling your reader carries with them after they close the book. With ChatGPT guiding your final strokes, you can land that ending in a way that's sharp, moving, and true to everything you've built.

A great ending does three key things. First, it resolves the main conflict. Second, it honors the emotional arc of your protagonist. And third, it reflects or resolves the central theme. Ask ChatGPT, "What emotional outcome should my protagonist reach if the theme is about finding self-worth?" and you'll get ideas for closing scenes that aren't just plot-conclusive, but emotionally resonant.

One way to start shaping your ending is to look back at your beginning. What was the first image, mood, or struggle we saw? A full-circle ending can be incredibly satisfying, not because everything is the same, but because we see how it has changed. If your story opened with a character alone, maybe it ends with them surrounded by people who truly see them. Ask ChatGPT, "How can I mirror the first chapter's opening image in a final scene to show transformation?" and you'll get beautiful symmetry that feels earned and intentional.

When it comes to resolving the main plot, think about the core question that's been driving the story. Did they find the killer? Did they escape? Did they win the race, save the relationship, uncover the truth? A satisfying ending answers that question—or subverts it in a way that still feels emotionally right. Even if the character fails, what matters is how they changed along the way. You can ask ChatGPT, "How can I end the story in a way that surprises the reader but still fits the character's arc?" and it will help you balance closure with freshness.

It's okay if some threads remain open—life is messy. But the emotional spine of the story must feel resolved. If your protagonist has been chasing forgiveness, we need a moment that reflects their ability to give or receive it. If they've been afraid of who they are, we need to see them own their truth. Ask ChatGPT, "Write a closing beat where the protagonist accepts themselves in a quiet, powerful way," and you'll get endings that land not with noise, but with emotional truth.

One of the most powerful ways to close a story is with a *choice*. Your protagonist makes a final decision that shows us who they are now—how they've grown, what they've learned, what they're willing to risk or let go of. Ask ChatGPT, "What choice could the main character make that reflects their full arc from fear to courage?" and you'll often uncover the perfect final action that locks everything in place.

Tone is everything in your final moments. If your story has been hopeful, leave the reader with a sense of rising light. If it's tragic, let the grief resonate without turning bleak. If it's uncertain, let the open door feel like possibility, not confusion. You can feed your last scene into ChatGPT and ask, "Does this ending match the emotional tone of the rest of the story?" and you'll get insight into whether your last note rings true or hits off-key.

Another elegant way to end a novel is with a callback—an object, phrase, place, or line of dialogue from earlier in the story that returns with new meaning. Maybe a character finally says the words they couldn't say before. Maybe they walk through the same door, but with a different heart. Ask ChatGPT, "What's a symbolic detail from earlier in the story that could return in the final scene for impact?" and you'll find ways to make your ending feel like a full circle without spelling it out.

Endings don't need to be long. Sometimes the most satisfying conclusions happen in a single page. A decision made, a truth acknowledged, a path walked. You can ask ChatGPT, "Write a one-paragraph closing scene that ends the story with emotional clarity," and you'll get a distilled version of your character's final beat—tight, focused, and powerful.

If you're writing genre fiction, there may be certain conventions to honor. A mystery needs to solve the puzzle. A romance needs to resolve the relationship. A thriller often demands a final confrontation. But even within genre, the best endings are the ones that surprise slightly while still feeling inevitable. You can prompt ChatGPT with, "What's a genre-appropriate ending for a story like this that avoids clichés?" and it will help you deliver something fresh but familiar.

Don't forget to think about what your ending *says*. What message are you leaving behind? What truth are you delivering in those final lines? Even if you've never stated your theme out loud, the ending is where it becomes clear. It's the answer to the question the story has been asking all along. Ask ChatGPT, "What final image or action could embody the theme of this novel without using dialogue?" and you'll get closing ideas that show, not tell.

If you're unsure whether your ending is hitting the mark, you can use ChatGPT as a test reader. Paste in your final scene and ask, "Does this ending feel emotionally satisfying and consistent with the character's journey?" You'll get honest feedback on tone, pacing, and closure—and suggestions for how to strengthen the ending without adding a lot of extra work.

And sometimes, the best closing line is one that opens something inside the reader. Not a door in the story, but a feeling, a thought, a pause. The kind of line that stays in someone's head long after the story is done. Ask ChatGPT, "Give me five final lines that feel open-ended but emotionally complete," and you'll likely find the perfect one waiting for you.

So as you write that final chapter in your one-day novel sprint, don't let exhaustion rob you of a strong ending. Let it be clear. Let it be true. Let it land like the last note of a beautiful song. Whether it's quiet or grand, peaceful or shattering, humorous or heartbreaking—if it feels *earned*, it will feel *right*.

That's how you write an ending that doesn't just finish a book—it completes it.

Revising and Editing with ChatGPT in Real Time

Writing a novel in one day is an adrenaline rush. You're flying through scenes, making snap decisions, and following your characters down twisting paths you might not have even planned. But once the words are on the page, the job isn't done—not if you want your story to really land. That's where revision and editing come in. And the beauty of working with ChatGPT is that you don't have to do it all alone. In fact, ChatGPT can act like your real-time editor, sounding board, line doctor, and structural analyst all in one. The secret is knowing how to ask—and how to let the AI sharpen what you've already created without flattening your voice.

The first thing to understand is that revising isn't about tearing everything down. It's about refining what's already working and tightening the parts that aren't quite there yet. When writing quickly, it's natural to overlook pacing bumps, repeated phrases, or undercooked dialogue. ChatGPT can spot these things in seconds. Just drop in a scene and ask, "Can you point out any weak spots or pacing issues in this chapter?" and you'll get a fast, focused review that saves you hours of guesswork.

Another incredibly helpful use of ChatGPT is clarifying your character arcs. You might have rushed through emotional beats, or maybe a turning point came too soon or didn't quite land. Copy a few key scenes into the chat and ask, "Does this character's emotional arc feel earned based on earlier scenes?" and ChatGPT will identify whether the growth feels natural or if it needs more setup. It can even suggest where to plant seeds for a stronger payoff later.

Let's talk about dialogue. In a writing sprint, dialogue is often where we fall back on placeholders or stiff exchanges just to keep moving. But you can revisit these lines and ask ChatGPT, "Can you make this conversation sound more natural and character-specific?" or "Rewrite this argument to be more emotionally intense without adding extra length." The AI will polish the rhythm, add nuance, and help differentiate character voices—fast.

If you're not sure whether a scene is doing enough for the plot, feed it into ChatGPT and ask, "What is the purpose of this scene? Is it moving the story forward?" This kind of real-time analysis gives you a fresh lens to evaluate your work without the tunnel vision that can come from speed-writing. You might discover that the scene works better as part of another, or that it needs an extra beat of conflict to truly earn its place.

One of the fastest editing tricks with ChatGPT is line tightening. If you've got chunky paragraphs that slow down the pace, just say, "Please rewrite this section to be more concise and keep the tone intact." In seconds, the AI will deliver a leaner version that maintains your intent but reads cleaner. You can do this chapter by chapter as you go, or circle back after the first draft is done.

Need to check consistency on the fly? ChatGPT is great at helping you catch details. Ask, "Did I mention earlier that this character had a brother? Is this line about her being an only child a mistake?" and it will scan the previous text and flag continuity errors. This is especially useful when you're working fast and haven't built a detailed reference sheet.

Pacing and tone can be tricky when you're writing fast. One chapter might feel slow and contemplative, while the next reads like an action movie. ChatGPT can help you regulate the flow. Feed in a chapter and ask, "Does this scene's tone match the previous one, or is the shift too abrupt?" It will give you honest feedback and offer suggestions to bridge tonal gaps without rewriting entire sections.

If you're revising an emotional scene, ask, "Can you enhance the emotional beats here without making it melodramatic?" or "What would make this moment more powerful without slowing the pacing?" ChatGPT can amplify what you've already written by pushing deeper into the emotional core of the moment—often with just a few added lines or stronger word choices.

One of the most powerful revision tools you have is **scene summary and intention**. Before editing a scene, ask ChatGPT, "Summarize what this scene is doing in one sentence. What changes by the end of it?" If the answer is vague or thin, you may need to rethink the purpose of the scene. You can also ask, "What's the central tension in this chapter, and how can I raise the stakes?" and you'll get targeted ways to add urgency or depth.

ChatGPT is also great for smoothing transitions. In a rush, it's easy to jump from scene to scene with abrupt breaks that disorient the reader. Drop in the last paragraph of one chapter and the first of the next and ask, "Can you write a transition paragraph that connects these two scenes smoothly?" and it'll give you a bridge that keeps the flow natural and immersive.

When you're editing dialogue-heavy scenes, you can also use ChatGPT to check balance. Ask, "Does this scene rely too much on dialogue? Should I add more action or internal thought?" It'll tell you where the rhythm feels static and offer suggestions to diversify the texture of the writing.

At the chapter level, you can run a quick health check by asking, "What are the high points and low points of tension in this chapter?" or "Is there a satisfying mini-arc in this section?" If a chapter feels flat, ask, "How can I rewrite this to end with more tension or a stronger emotional beat?" ChatGPT will help you insert small hooks or adjustments that elevate the chapter instantly.

One of the best parts of using ChatGPT in real-time revision is that you never have to second-guess whether a sentence works or not. If you feel stuck on a line, just say, "Give me three variations of this sentence that sound more poetic" or "Rewrite this in a more sarcastic tone." You'll get options immediately, and sometimes, the AI's phrasing sparks a better version you hadn't even considered.

And when it comes time for final polish, ask ChatGPT, "Can you do a style pass on this page for voice, tone, and clarity?" and let it tune the language without flattening your style. You're not handing off creative control—you're using AI as a focused, fast, intelligent writing partner who never tires of line edits.

The beauty of revising with ChatGPT isn't just about fixing mistakes—it's about *elevating* your story in ways that keep it yours, just better. Faster. Clearer. More compelling.

So don't wait until tomorrow or next week to fix your draft. Do it in real time. Bounce ideas off the AI. Sharpen scenes while the story is still hot in your mind. Keep your momentum alive, and let revision become part of your writing flow, not something you dread after the sprint ends.

That's how you write a book in one day—and *make it feel like it took weeks.*

Self-Critiquing Your AI-Written Work

Writing a novel in a single day with ChatGPT is exhilarating. You race through chapters, ideas flow easily, and before you know it, you've got a full book in your hands. But once the adrenaline fades and the dust settles, it's time for the most essential and underrated part of the process—stepping back and taking a hard, honest look at what you've created. Not to beat yourself up, but to strengthen the work. Not to judge the speed, but to judge the story. This is where self-critiquing comes in. And even though you used AI to help write it, you, the human, are still the author. So it's your responsibility to make sure it's not just fast—but good.

Self-critiquing isn't about being ruthless. It's about being intentional. And the first thing you should do is distance yourself just a little from the excitement of having "finished." Close the document for a few hours—or even a full day if you've got the time—and come back with fresh eyes. If you're reviewing in real time, take a chapter break, stand up, walk around, and then read like a reader, not like the writer who just typed "The End."

Start by asking the big questions. Does this story make sense from beginning to end? Does it build emotionally and narratively in a way that feels satisfying? If you aren't sure, summarize the book in a few sentences and ask yourself: is this the book I meant to write? If your summary sounds like a different story than what's on the page, you've drifted somewhere in the writing. That's okay—but it's a sign you might need to revise toward clarity.

When reviewing AI-written sections, pay attention to **consistency**. AI can sometimes forget things mid-way through—maybe a character's eye color changes, or a plot point vanishes. These aren't big problems, but you have to be the one who notices. Read each chapter with a mental checklist: are the character motivations consistent? Are the facts about the world or events of the plot lining up? You can use ChatGPT to help here—paste a chapter and ask, "Does anything in this chapter contradict earlier events?" and let it help you cross-check.

Voice is another big area for self-critique. Sometimes AI writing can start to sound a little generic or even sterile, especially if you didn't give it detailed stylistic instructions. Reread your scenes and ask yourself: does this sound like *me*? Does this feel emotionally honest? If something feels flat, highlight it and ask ChatGPT, "Can you rewrite this paragraph in a voice that's more intimate/playful/dark/sarcastic?" Use the AI to shape the tone you actually want, not just the one you got on the first try.

Keep an eye out for **repetition**. AI tends to reuse certain sentence structures, phrases, or word choices. You might find that characters nod too often, or that every chapter ends with someone staring into the distance. These small tics can dull the energy of the story. Skim your paragraphs and look for visual or verbal patterns. Ask yourself: do these moments stand out or blend into each other? Then go back and tweak. Or feed it into ChatGPT and say, "Can you remove repetition and vary the sentence rhythm while keeping the meaning?"

Emotional beats deserve your close attention, too. It's easy, especially when writing fast, to glide over huge emotional shifts with a line or two. But those are the moments where your reader connects. When a character is heartbroken, betrayed, elated, terrified—does the moment land? Reread those key scenes slowly. Ask yourself: did I feel this? If not, ask ChatGPT, "How can I deepen the emotional response in this scene without making it overdramatic?" and see if the suggestions help draw out more depth and realism.

Now turn to pacing. One of the telltale signs of an AI-assisted draft is uneven pacing—some chapters move too quickly, others linger too long. Read your book like a reader would. Are there moments where it drags? Where things happen too fast to care? Make notes. Then ask ChatGPT, "How can I add tension to this slow section?" or "How can I slow down this scene to make it more meaningful?" The AI won't just point out the issue—it'll help you solve it.

Another great trick is to read your dialogue out loud. If it sounds stiff, overly formal, or like the same person is speaking through every character, that's a flag. Ask yourself: does this sound like real people talking? Does each character have a unique way of speaking? If not, copy a snippet of dialogue and ask ChatGPT, "Can you rewrite this conversation so each character's voice is more distinct?" and you'll get dialogue that feels truer to the character's identity.

Don't forget structure. Even if your story moves fast and hits the big beats, you want to double-check that your three acts hold together. Did your story escalate in the middle? Did the midpoint twist shake things up? Did the climax pay off the story's central tension? If anything feels out of place or underdeveloped, ask ChatGPT, "Does this story follow a clear three-act structure, and where can I strengthen the transitions between acts?" You'll get structural insights that can guide your final polish.

If you're not sure what's missing but you can feel something's off, zoom out and ask bigger questions:

Does the protagonist change?

Is there a clear emotional or thematic throughline?

Does the ending feel earned?

Feed ChatGPT a brief summary of your plot and ask, "What could be missing to make this story more emotionally satisfying?" or "What loose ends could I resolve for a stronger ending?" These kinds of questions help you see what's not yet on the page—but could be.

Finally, listen to your gut. If something feels flat, weird, too convenient, or "not quite right," even if you can't explain why—trust that. Your reader will feel it too. Use ChatGPT to workshop alternatives. "This scene feels off—can you offer three different versions with higher stakes?" Let the AI give you fresh options, and pick the one that clicks.

Self-critiquing doesn't mean tearing your draft apart—it means *fine-tuning the instrument*. You've got the melody, the rhythm, the lyrics. Now it's time to tighten the strings, adjust the pitch, and bring out the harmony that was always there.

With ChatGPT by your side, you've got the tools to write fast—but also to revise smart. So take a breath, look at what you've created, and don't be afraid to push it one step further. Not because it wasn't good—but because it can be *great*.

Getting the Tone and Voice Right from the Start

Tone and voice are what make your story *yours*. They're the flavor, the texture, the sound of your storytelling that lingers in a reader's mind even after they've forgotten the plot. The tone sets the mood—lighthearted or brooding, romantic or cynical, playful or tense. The voice is how you say what you say—through word choice, rhythm, personality, and attitude. And when you get them right from the very first page, everything else in your novel flows with more confidence and clarity. When writing a book in one day with ChatGPT, locking in tone and voice early is one of the smartest moves you can make.

It starts with knowing what kind of *feeling* you want your book to give off. Is it gritty and raw? Smooth and poetic? Snarky and sarcastic? Warm and comforting? You can ask ChatGPT right at the planning stage: "Help me define the tone for a coming-of-age story with bittersweet humor," and you'll get suggestions that give your book an emotional compass before you even write the first line.

Voice is a bit trickier—it's part style, part personality, and part point of view. It might come from the narrator or be rooted in the protagonist's inner world. A cynical detective novel has a very different voice than a dreamy fantasy story told by a teenage girl discovering magic. One is probably punchy, short, and dark. The other might be poetic, whimsical, or wide-eyed. You can test this with ChatGPT by saying, "Write a paragraph in the voice of a sarcastic thief narrating their own heist," or "Try this scene in the tone of a noir film," and you'll see what kinds of choices shape tone and voice in action.

If you're unsure how your story *should* sound, try experimenting in different voices before you commit. Take a single scene and ask ChatGPT to write it in three styles: formal and literary, casual and comedic, and moody and introspective. Read each version out loud and feel which one fits your story world best. That's how you tune your ear to the right narrative frequency.

Getting the tone and voice right early also helps you stay consistent—especially when you're writing fast. Once your story knows how it sounds, it won't keep shifting tones mid-chapter. That's where ChatGPT becomes a valuable real-time assistant. After you've written a few paragraphs or pages, ask, "Does this sample maintain a consistent tone?" or "How can I adjust the voice to make it more confident and character-driven?" and you'll get focused tips that help you tighten your style.

Let's talk about **opening tone**, because that's your handshake with the reader. The first few lines of your novel do more than introduce plot—they whisper to the reader: "This is what kind of ride you're in for." So make sure that first paragraph reflects the *emotional color* of your book. Ask ChatGPT, "Write three possible opening paragraphs for a horror novel with a poetic tone," and choose the one that sets the right vibe.

Voice also includes **point of view**—and this is a huge stylistic choice. First person tends to be more intimate, emotional, and voice-heavy. Third person can be flexible—close, distant, omniscient—but the voice still needs to feel unified. If you're writing in first person, ChatGPT can help you define that voice early by prompting: "Write a first-person paragraph in the voice of a character who hides pain behind humor." What comes back can serve as a style guide you follow throughout the book.

Your protagonist's personality can shape voice even when the story isn't told in first person. A close third-person narration can still carry their filter. Their fears, beliefs, and humor can subtly bleed into the way the world is described.

Ask ChatGPT, "How would a nervous, overly analytical character describe walking into a bar?" and the answer will show how to align your voice with character perspective.

Tone also affects your *sentence style*. A romantic tone might use long, lyrical sentences. A thriller might lean on short, sharp bursts. A quirky comedy might be full of odd metaphors or unexpected phrasing. You can ask ChatGPT, "Adjust this paragraph to match a whimsical tone without losing the plot details," and you'll see how changing a few words or rhythms transforms the feel of the text.

As you write, keep checking in with your tone. Does a dark, emotional moment suddenly feel jokey? Is a tender scene slipping into melodrama? ChatGPT can help keep your tone in check. Say, "Does this scene match the established tone of the story?" or "How can I revise this to make it feel more sincere and less over-the-top?" and it'll offer constructive ideas, not just critiques.

One smart move is to create a *voice and tone profile* at the very start of your writing sprint. Jot down some words that describe how your story should feel—like "melancholy but hopeful," "sardonic and fast-paced," or "mysterious and dreamlike." Then, when in doubt, run a piece of your writing through ChatGPT and ask, "Does this paragraph match the profile 'sardonic and fast-paced'?" That little check-in can save you a lot of backtracking later.

If you feel like your voice is drifting, don't panic. Take a break, go back to a strong chapter or paragraph that *does* sound right, and use it as a tuning fork. Or ask ChatGPT, "Remind me what stylistic choices I used earlier to create a tense but humorous tone?" and get a quick recap of your own writing style.

Tone and voice are what readers remember. Plot might grab them, but voice keeps them reading—and tone makes them feel something. Whether it's the dry humor of your main character or the moody atmosphere that hangs over every chapter, these elements are the emotional foundation of your book.

So don't wait until the editing phase to worry about tone and voice. Set them from the first line. Let them guide your choices, scene by scene. And when you get stuck, turn to ChatGPT—not just as a plot helper, but as a tone technician and voice coach. Because when your story *sounds* right, everything else starts to fall into place.

That's how you keep your reader not just reading—but *listening*.

Writing in Different Tenses and Points of View with Ease

Tense and point of view are like the lens and lighting in a film—they shape how your reader experiences the story. Whether you write in first person present tense or third person past, that choice instantly affects the intimacy, immediacy, and emotional feel of your novel. When you're writing an entire fiction book in a single day with ChatGPT, locking into the right tense and point of view early makes the whole writing process smoother. But it's also freeing to know that you can switch, experiment, or adjust them at any time with confidence—because ChatGPT can help you do it with ease and consistency.

Let's start with tense. You've got two main options—**past tense** and **present tense**. Past tense is the classic default. It feels natural, familiar, and works well for both intimate and distant narration. It gives the sense that the story has already happened, which can create authority and reflection. Present tense, on the other hand, is immediate and visceral. Everything feels like it's unfolding in real time. It can be more intense, more breathless, and often puts the reader right in the protagonist's skin.

Neither is better—they just do different things. You can ask ChatGPT something like, "What are the pros and cons of writing a thriller in present tense vs. past tense?" and it'll give you a quick breakdown to help you decide. Once you're clear on the effect you want, commit early. But if you find yourself drifting mid-draft, don't worry—you can paste a scene in and say, "Convert this from past tense to present tense while keeping the tone intact," and ChatGPT will rewrite it for you on the spot.

What matters most is consistency. Switching tenses mid-story (unless it's intentional for effect) is one of the quickest ways to confuse a reader. After your first few chapters, you can check yourself by asking ChatGPT, "Scan this scene and tell me if all the verbs are in the correct tense." It'll catch anything that slipped through in the rush of writing.

Now let's talk point of view. The most common ones in fiction are **first person**, **third person limited**, and **third person omniscient**.

First person ("I walked into the room...") creates deep intimacy. You're living inside the character's head, experiencing the world as they do, including all their biases, blind spots, and emotions. This is great for character-driven stories or emotionally raw narratives. It lets your protagonist speak directly to the reader. You can tell ChatGPT, "Write this scene in first person from the point of view of someone trying to hide their fear," and it'll show you how to capture voice and internal tension.

Third person limited ("She walked into the room...") gives you a bit more distance, but still allows you to stay close to one character's perspective. It's versatile and lets you describe things the character wouldn't describe themselves. You can use it for a broader narrative while keeping emotional depth. If you've started your novel in first person but want a bit more flexibility, paste a chapter into ChatGPT and ask, "Rewrite this in third person limited without losing the emotional tone," and you'll see exactly how it translates.

Third person omniscient zooms out even more. You can jump between characters, reveal information the protagonist doesn't know, and comment on the story from a god-like distance. This style gives you big-picture control, but if not handled carefully, it can feel detached. ChatGPT can help you learn how to use it properly. Ask, "How can I shift from limited third to omniscient smoothly in this scene without confusing the reader?" and it will guide you through the transition.

There's also **second person** ("You walk into the room...") which is rare, but very powerful when used well—especially in experimental fiction, immersive thrillers, or introspective stories where the reader becomes the protagonist. You can try, "Write a scene in second person where the character realizes they've been betrayed," and ChatGPT will show you how different the tone becomes with that choice.

The best way to choose point of view is to ask yourself: *Whose story is this, and how close do I want the reader to feel to them?* If you want the reader inside the main character's skin, go first person or close third. If you want to show how the entire world is affected by a single event, consider omniscient. Once you pick a POV, make sure it's clear and steady. ChatGPT can help you lock it in by scanning your work and flagging any shifts or inconsistencies.

One smart move is to create a POV cheat sheet. You can ask ChatGPT, "Give me a checklist of things to keep consistent when writing in first person present tense," and you'll get reminders about verb choices, internal narration, filtering language ("I saw," "I noticed"), and staying in the character's head. This kind of reference helps you stay sharp while writing fast.

Sometimes, writers want to switch POVs in the same novel—especially in ensemble stories or dual timelines. That's totally doable as long as you're deliberate. Use clear scene or chapter breaks and make sure each POV character has a distinct voice and viewpoint. Ask ChatGPT, "Help me create two distinct character voices for alternating first-person chapters," and you'll get style tips, emotional cues, and vocabulary choices to keep them from sounding the same.

If you're editing a draft and realize the story would be stronger in a different tense or POV, don't panic. Copy a scene and say, "Can you convert this to third person past tense and shift the perspective to another character?" ChatGPT will make the change instantly—saving you hours of mechanical rewriting and letting you focus on shaping the new emotional rhythm.

Voice is also linked to POV. A sarcastic first-person narrator will color every sentence with attitude. A reserved third-person narrator might be more observant and distant. Let ChatGPT help you refine this by prompting, "Rewrite this scene in first person with a bitter, self-deprecating tone," and it'll show you how voice and POV work together to shape the entire reading experience.

In the end, writing in different tenses and points of view isn't about rules—it's about control. You get to decide how close the reader stands to the story. You decide what they know, what they don't, and how they feel about it. And with ChatGPT's ability to switch gears quickly and guide your revisions on the fly, you can experiment freely, adjust easily, and lock into a style that feels right.

So don't be afraid to try different lenses. Find the one that makes your story come alive. And once you find it, use it with confidence—because now you've got the tools to keep it consistent, clean, and compelling, even when you're writing at lightning speed.

Using ChatGPT for Internal Monologues and Deep Thoughts

One of the most powerful tools in fiction is the inner life of your characters—the thoughts they don't say out loud, the fears they hide, the questions they ask themselves in the middle of quiet moments or intense action. These internal monologues are where characters become *real*. Readers connect most deeply not when something explodes, but when a character reflects, doubts, hopes, or breaks down quietly. And when you're writing a full novel in one day, using ChatGPT to craft those internal monologues and deep thoughts can elevate your story from entertaining to unforgettable.

Internal monologue is the private conversation a character has with themselves. It reveals emotion, values, regrets, confusion, and raw honesty in a way that dialogue and action often can't. Whether your story is in first person, close third, or even second person, showing your character's inner voice adds layers and makes every moment feel personal.

To write internal monologue well, you need to go beneath the surface of what's happening. If a character is running from danger, what are they *really* thinking? Are they scared of dying—or of never proving themselves? Are they angry at someone who abandoned them—or ashamed of what they've become? You can ask ChatGPT, "What would a character think during a high-stakes chase if they feel betrayed by a close friend?" and it will give you emotional context to weave into the action.

You can also use ChatGPT to go deeper into emotional transitions. Say your character just experienced a loss. You might write a scene where they cry, drink, or lash out. But the gold is in what they *tell themselves* in those moments—the lies, the denial, the memories. Ask ChatGPT, "Give me a stream-of-consciousness paragraph for a character trying to convince themselves they're fine after losing someone," and you'll get emotionally rich monologue that doesn't feel forced or expositional.

Internal thoughts are also a great way to explore contradictions. Humans are messy. A character might act brave while thinking, *I have no idea what I'm doing.* They might help someone while resenting them. They might fall in love while trying to talk themselves out of it. These contrasts create realism. Try prompting ChatGPT with, "Write an internal monologue for a character who's in love but doesn't want to admit it," and you'll get nuance that lifts your romance above cliché.

Internal monologue isn't just about emotion—it's also a tool for **voice**. The way a character thinks should sound different from the way another character thinks. One might overanalyze everything. Another might be blunt and sarcastic. You can fine-tune character voice with prompts like, "Give me a bitter, sarcastic internal monologue from a character who hates their job but is pretending everything's fine," and let ChatGPT help you lock in a distinct rhythm and tone.

Another strength of internal monologue is how it controls **pacing**. In a tense scene, slipping into a character's head slows things down and deepens the impact. Right before a character pulls a trigger, says "I love you," or opens a long-lost letter, you can insert a few lines of thought to stretch the moment. Ask ChatGPT, "Write a slow, tense internal thought sequence before a character makes a life-changing decision," and use those lines to build pressure before the release.

You can also use internal monologue to deliver **backstory** organically. Rather than dumping exposition into dialogue, let a character remember, reflect, or rationalize. Maybe they see a scar and recall the night they got it. Maybe a voice reminds them of someone they failed to save. Ask ChatGPT, "How can I write a paragraph of internal thought that reveals a traumatic event without explaining too much?" and you'll get subtle ways to hint at the past while staying grounded in the present.

Don't forget that internal monologue can be humorous too. If your story has a sarcastic or witty narrator, the inner voice becomes the source of some of the best comedy. You can write a completely normal scene—buying coffee, waiting in line—and make it hilarious just by showing what the character's thinking the whole time. ChatGPT is excellent at helping with this. Try, "Write a funny inner monologue for a character stuck in a painfully awkward social situation," and you'll get gold.

There's also the tool of **contradiction between action and thought**. A character might smile while thinking, *I'd rather punch you in the face*. This builds tension and dramatic irony, because the reader knows the truth even if the other characters don't. Prompt ChatGPT with, "Give me an example of a polite conversation where the inner monologue is totally at odds with the dialogue," and use the result to show hidden emotion and conflict.

When writing fast, it's easy to rush through events and forget the weight those moments carry. Internal monologue slows you down just enough to show what your characters are processing—without breaking the flow. After you finish a chapter, you can ask ChatGPT, "Where could I insert internal thoughts to make this scene more emotional or immersive?" and it'll suggest specific points where a pause in the character's head would add impact.

You can even use inner monologue structurally. Start each chapter with a short internal reflection. End a major scene with a question only the character is asking themselves. These threads create continuity. Ask ChatGPT, "Give me a recurring internal question that evolves with the character across the story," and you'll have a motif that carries emotional weight all the way to the end.

If you're ever unsure whether your monologue is hitting the right note, copy a section and say, "Does this internal monologue feel honest, or does it sound forced?" ChatGPT can tell you where to cut, reword, or expand. It might even suggest a stronger emotional throughline you didn't realize was there.

Ultimately, internal monologues are what make characters *human*. They take the reader behind the curtain and say, "Here's what I'm really feeling." Whether it's doubt, desire, rage, guilt, hope, or confusion, these inner voices invite empathy—and empathy is what turns a fast-paced story into a meaningful one.

So don't be afraid to slow down and dive inside your character's head. Use ChatGPT to workshop the emotions, refine the phrasing, and explore the psychology. Whether you're adding a single line of thought or a full paragraph of stream-of-consciousness, you're giving your reader something deeper than plot—you're giving them connection. And that's what fiction is really for.

Keeping Your Story Cohesive in a Rush

Writing a complete novel in one day sounds like a mad dash—and in some ways, it is. The clock is ticking, the word count is rising, and you're trying to move from one scene to the next without falling into chaos. But even in a rapid writing session, your story still needs to *hang together*. It needs structure, flow, and a clear emotional journey. Readers shouldn't feel the rush—they should feel the rhythm. The good news is, you don't need to slow down to create cohesion. With ChatGPT as your co-writer and guide, you can write fast and still stay focused, tight, and connected from start to finish.

Cohesion starts with clarity. Before you type your first line, take five minutes to nail down three core things: your protagonist, your main conflict, and the emotional or thematic arc. These are your story's anchors. Everything else can flex, change, or surprise you—but these should stay clear throughout. You can tell ChatGPT, "Help me summarize my story in one sentence," or "What's the emotional transformation my protagonist should go through?" This keeps your vision sharp even when the scenes start flying.

One of the fastest ways a rushed story can unravel is when the pacing gets choppy. You might have three intense scenes in a row and then pages of wandering setup, or you might skip crucial development just to reach the ending. Cohesion comes from *momentum*, not just speed. Ask ChatGPT, "Does my outline have a good balance of tension, development, and payoff?" and it can help you rearrange or add beats so the flow feels natural.

A huge part of writing fast but cohesively is **scene transitions**. When writing quickly, it's easy to jump from moment to moment without clear bridges, which leaves readers disoriented. But you don't need elaborate transitions—you just need a sentence or two to reorient the reader in time, space, or emotion. ChatGPT can do this effortlessly. Just say, "Write a quick, natural transition between a fight scene and a quiet reflection moment," and it'll give you options that keep the tone and flow intact.

Another tool for cohesion is the **emotional thread**. Your character doesn't just move through plot points—they carry emotional weight with them. If they're heartbroken in chapter three, that sadness should echo in chapter four. If they've been betrayed, that suspicion should color their next choices. You can ask ChatGPT, "How can I show emotional continuity for a character who's just experienced a major loss?" and it'll give you subtle beats, reactions, or thoughts to layer in and keep the character's experience consistent.

Keeping a cohesive voice also helps your story feel whole. Whether you're writing in first person, third person, present or past tense, you want the narration to *sound* the same throughout. One common pitfall in rushed writing is accidental tone shifts. A serious thriller starts sounding like a rom-com halfway through. If you're unsure, you can paste a few chapters into ChatGPT and ask, "Does this sample maintain a consistent tone and voice?" It will spot tonal shifts and help you recalibrate.

Another trick for staying cohesive is using **repetition with variation**. A phrase, image, or idea that shows up more than once—at the beginning, middle, and end—gives your story structure without requiring you to micromanage it. For example, a character might keep recalling a childhood memory that changes meaning over time. Ask ChatGPT, "What image or line can I repeat throughout the book to create emotional unity?" and you'll get motifs that echo through the story and give it shape.

Chapter structure is your friend, too. Try keeping each chapter focused on a clear purpose: a decision, a discovery, a relationship shift, or a rise in tension. Even when you're writing fast, if every chapter has a "point," your story won't wander. You can ask ChatGPT, "What's the core function of this chapter in the overall story arc?" and it'll help you cut fluff and stay on track.

Dialogue is another place cohesion can slip. In a rush, characters might start sounding the same or the conversations might drift without a clear goal. Every bit of dialogue should either reveal something, escalate something, or move something. If a scene feels flat, feed it to ChatGPT and ask, "How can I revise this conversation to reflect the story's main conflict?" The AI will point you toward stronger emotional or narrative links.

Let's not forget subplots. They add richness, but if they're not tied to the main arc, they can derail your momentum. ChatGPT can help you course-correct quickly. Ask, "How can I tie this romantic subplot into the character's journey of self-worth?" and it'll show you how to link emotional beats so the subplot feels like it belongs.

Even your setting and descriptions can be used to unify the story. A recurring location, a certain weather pattern, or symbolic object can anchor your scenes visually and emotionally. Ask ChatGPT, "What kind of recurring setting detail can reflect my character's inner state as they change?" and use it as a visual thread that carries across chapters.

If at any point you feel like your story is unraveling, just pause and zoom out. Ask ChatGPT for a **quick summary of what's happened so far**, and then compare that to your ending. Say, "Here's where we are. How do I get to the ending from here without rushing or derailing the arc?" and it will map out a few scenes or emotional beats that bridge the gap.

And if you're really unsure whether everything fits, you can do a real-time "cohesion check." Paste a page or two and ask, "Does this scene feel like a natural continuation of the previous one? Are the character's actions and emotions consistent?" ChatGPT will not only tell you—it'll suggest edits on the spot.

In the end, writing fast doesn't mean sacrificing quality. It means being efficient, focused, and clear about what the story is *about* at every stage. Cohesion doesn't come from slowing down—it comes from being intentional. With ChatGPT helping you stay grounded, connecting emotional threads, smoothing transitions, and sharpening scenes, you can keep your story tight even when you're racing the clock.

So take a breath, stay connected to your core idea, and let the pieces come together. A cohesive story doesn't just feel complete—it *feels right*. And with the right tools in your hands, you can write one in a single day and still make it feel like it took a month to craft.

Using Images to Inspire Writing Prompts

Sometimes a single image can do what paragraphs of description can't—it can spark a world, breathe life into a character, or ignite a scene you didn't know you needed. When you're writing a novel in one day, staying creatively fueled is everything. And one of the best shortcuts to fresh, imaginative material is visual inspiration. Whether you're working from a photo, digital art, AI-generated image, or even a painting, you can use pictures as jumping-off points for rich, fast storytelling. And with ChatGPT, turning those visuals into dynamic writing prompts becomes effortless.

Images bypass your logic and go straight to your intuition. You don't need to analyze or explain them—they just hit you. A crumbling tower in the mist might immediately suggest a haunted backstory. A lone figure under neon lights might whisper of noir, secrets, or cyberpunk futures. These immediate associations are gold when you're trying to write fast and need strong, grounded ideas.

Start with a simple exercise: find or create an image—any image that makes you feel something. Then ask ChatGPT, "Describe this image in vivid sensory detail as if it were the opening of a novel." You'll get a paragraph that instantly sets mood, tone, and place. From there, you can keep asking: "Who is the person in this scene?" "What are they feeling?" "Why are they here?" and a whole world starts to take shape without overthinking.

One way to build a whole book off an image is to reverse-engineer your story from the visual. Let's say you have an image of a broken-down android in a field of flowers. That's not just a moment—it's a mystery. Ask ChatGPT, "Give me five story ideas based on this image," and you'll get different angles: a robot discovering consciousness, a lost war machine reclaiming peace, a scientist searching for a runaway AI. Each prompt becomes a doorway to a full novel if you follow it.

You can even write backwards using images. Find a compelling final scene—a dramatic sunset with a figure walking into the sea, or a throne room covered in blood and roses—and ask, "What story could lead to this moment?" ChatGPT will give you a plot that climbs toward the visual climax, helping you shape the rest of your book with clarity and tension.

Images also work wonders for **character creation**. Zoom in on a person's face, posture, clothing, or surroundings in a photo. Ask ChatGPT, "Create a character profile based on this person. What's their job, secret, emotional wound, and personal goal?" and you'll receive a full sketch ready to drop into your story. You can build a love interest, villain, sidekick, or protagonist this way in minutes.

Let's say you find a landscape that strikes you—a foggy forest, a neon-lit alleyway, a ruined cathedral. Ask ChatGPT, "What type of story or genre would best match this image?" and you'll get ideas for horror, romance, mystery, or fantasy that match the aesthetic. Then follow up with, "Write the first paragraph of a novel set in this location," and suddenly you're not staring at a blank page anymore.

You can also string multiple images together for **story mapping**. Try this: choose three random visuals—a setting, a character, and an object. Maybe it's a snowy village, a woman with a mechanical arm, and a shattered hourglass. Feed them into ChatGPT and say, "Give me a plot outline using these three elements," and you'll get a surprising, imaginative thread tying everything together. It's fast. It's flexible. It works.

If you're already partway into your novel and feel stuck, use an image to reinvigorate your scenes. Ask ChatGPT, "Insert a new image-based element into this chapter to raise the stakes," and it might suggest a mysterious stranger entering, a storm approaching, or an object being discovered. The new visual twist adds depth and helps you avoid writing scenes that feel static or predictable.

Visuals are also a great way to spark **emotion**. A tender image—two hands touching through glass, a child sitting alone on a swing, a soldier looking at an old photo—can inspire internal monologues, memory flashbacks, or relationship moments. Prompt ChatGPT with, "Write an emotional scene inspired by this image," and it will give you something with resonance and heart that ties into your theme or character arc.

Even dialogue can be born from images. Show a picture of two people facing each other, and ask ChatGPT, "What are these characters saying? What's the tension between them?" You'll get rich, layered exchanges that feel alive and urgent. This is perfect when you want to avoid filler and write conversations that *matter*.

If you're visually inclined, you can even generate your own AI images using platforms like DALL·E, Midjourney, or Artbreeder. Once you've got the image, just say, "Write a scene based on this visual," and let ChatGPT build the setting, characters, and mood from what it sees. It's like storyboarding in reverse.

And if you want to really get experimental, try using images to create story *structure*. Choose four to six pictures that feel connected—beginning, middle, and end. Ask ChatGPT, "Create a novel outline that connects these six images as key scenes in a story," and you'll have a loose map that still leaves room for discovery but keeps your narrative cohesive.

The truth is, you don't need a perfect idea to start writing—you just need a *spark*. Images give you that spark instantly. They shortcut your brain's resistance and feed your imagination directly. Combined with ChatGPT's ability to interpret, expand, and structure those ideas, you can turn any visual into an entire world on the page.

So whether you're stuck, rushed, or just want something new to play with, let images lead the way. Find a face, a place, a moment frozen in time. Ask the right questions. Let ChatGPT pull the thread. And before you know it, you're writing not from scratch—but from something alive, atmospheric, and already half-story.

Because sometimes the fastest way to find the words... is to *see* them first.

How to Use ChatGPT to Mirror Your Personal Style

One of the biggest concerns writers have when using AI is losing their own voice. After all, what's the point of writing a novel—especially in a single day—if it doesn't sound like *you*? The good news is that with a few smart tricks and some upfront guidance, ChatGPT can absolutely learn to mirror your style. Not just your vocabulary or sentence structure, but your tone, rhythm, attitude, and overall storytelling vibe. The AI isn't here to replace your voice—it's here to *amplify* it. And once it knows what you sound like, it can help you write faster and more confidently without ever feeling like a robot co-wrote your story.

The key to teaching ChatGPT your style is showing it—not telling it. Start by writing a paragraph or two in your own voice. It could be from a past project, a journal entry, or just something you improvise on the spot. Then feed it to ChatGPT and say, "This is my writing style. Analyze the tone, vocabulary, and sentence structure, and describe it back to me." You'll get a breakdown of how you write—maybe you use short, clipped sentences, maybe you like poetic phrasing, or maybe you have a dry sense of humor tucked between every line.

Once you know how the AI interprets your style, you can reinforce it by giving clear instructions. For example: "Write this chapter in a voice that's casual, introspective, and slightly sarcastic—like the sample I gave you." You can also say things like, "Use short paragraphs, avoid long exposition, and lean into emotional subtext." The more specific you are, the better the result.

The next trick is tone matching. If you've written a few chapters already, you can copy and paste a section into ChatGPT and ask, "Can you match this tone and continue the next paragraph in the same voice?" It will study your rhythm and structure, then write in a way that flows seamlessly from what you've already created. If the tone starts drifting later on, you can always pull it back by re-feeding your earlier chapters as style references.

If you want to shape ChatGPT's voice into something truly unique, combine your writing with a few outside influences. Say you love your own witty tone, but also admire the sharp dialogue of Elmore Leonard or the moody prose of Gillian Flynn. You can say, "Write this in my style, but let it borrow the pacing and edge of a noir thriller," and it will blend those qualities while staying rooted in your personal voice.

It also helps to define a few *style rules* for your project. These are small things that, together, define your writing fingerprint. Maybe you always open chapters with one-line hooks. Maybe you avoid semicolons. Maybe your dialogue is punchy and full of interruption. Give those rules to ChatGPT and say, "Stick to these stylistic choices throughout the novel," and it will follow your lead faithfully.

Another great tool is using ChatGPT for rewriting or polishing without sacrificing voice. Let's say you wrote a rough paragraph that you love emotionally but it needs tightening. Instead of rewriting it completely, say, "Rewrite this paragraph to be smoother and more vivid, but keep the original tone and sentence structure." ChatGPT will offer variations that sharpen your ideas while keeping the soul of the original intact.

Sometimes it's helpful to ask ChatGPT to *evaluate* your style. Paste a scene and ask, "Does this read consistently with the rest of my book? Are there any spots where the tone slips?" It will point out sections that feel off and suggest how to bring them back in line without flattening your voice.

You can also teach ChatGPT how your characters speak. If you have a main character with a specific way of thinking or speaking—like fast-paced internal monologue, dark humor, or poetic reflections—give ChatGPT a few examples and say, "This is how my protagonist talks. Use this voice for all of their narration and dialogue." As the story progresses, the AI will maintain that consistency and help deepen the character's unique style.

If you've never defined your personal style before, ChatGPT can help you figure it out. Paste in a chapter and ask, "What's distinctive about this writing style? What elements make it stand out?" You'll get an objective look at your strengths, whether it's your use of metaphor, your emotional honesty, or the way you build tension through quiet moments. Once you know your style signatures, you can lean into them even more.

And if you want to try something completely new—like writing in a gritty thriller tone when you usually do romantic comedies—you can say, "Take my normal style and darken the tone for a suspense novel. Keep my sentence rhythm but add tension and edge." This lets you experiment without losing your natural flow.

It's important to remember that ChatGPT doesn't have its own agenda. It doesn't *want* your story to sound generic. It only writes that way if you don't give it guidance. When you shape it with your voice, it will follow your lead. The more you feed it samples, reminders, and requests, the more it becomes a reflection of your unique storytelling DNA.

So as you're writing your one-day novel, let ChatGPT handle the heavy lifting of word count, transitions, and filler, while you stay focused on keeping the heart of the story *yours*. Your voice is the soul of your book. The AI is just the instrument. And once it's tuned to your pitch, you'll be amazed at how fluently it can sing in your key.

This is how you write fast *and* stay authentic. No compromise. No cut corners. Just you—amplified.

Mixing Genres and Making It Work

Genre is what gives readers expectations—and mixing genres is what gives them surprises. When you combine genres well, you create a story that feels fresh, layered, and completely your own. But when you mix them poorly, it can feel messy or directionless. The key to getting it right is understanding what each genre brings to the table, deciding what you want to borrow, and making sure it all serves a single, unified story. When you're writing a novel in one day with ChatGPT, you don't have time for second-guessing. So let's talk about how to mix genres with purpose, clarity, and a whole lot of creative firepower.

First things first—what does it actually mean to "mix genres"? You're basically combining two or more story types to create a hybrid. Maybe it's a sci-fi romance. Maybe it's a murder mystery set in a fantasy world. Maybe it's a comedy about time-traveling lawyers. You take familiar elements from each genre—like magic, suspense, romance, action, or satire—and find a way to blend them without losing the emotional center of your story.

The first step is choosing your base genre—the one that will ground the story's *structure*. This is usually what drives the plot. If it's a mystery, the story revolves around a question. If it's a romance, the central arc is about a relationship. If it's horror, then the mood and stakes are defined by fear. Ask ChatGPT, "Which genre should I use as the core structure for a story that mixes romance and time travel?" and it'll help you pick the right foundation to build on.

Once you know the base, you can layer in the second genre. This one adds color, tone, texture, and theme. Let's say you're writing a thriller that also has strong comedy. The structure follows the tension and danger of the thriller, but the tone is infused with wit, awkwardness, or absurdity. Or maybe you're writing a dystopian sci-fi with a deep romance at the heart—then your plot might be driven by rebellion and survival, but the emotional arc comes from the love story.

One trick that helps keep things cohesive is deciding what *role* each genre plays. Is one driving the action while the other deepens the theme? Is one shaping the world while the other defines character goals? You can ask ChatGPT, "How can I balance horror and fantasy so that the horror shapes the tone and the fantasy builds the world?" and it'll give you a framework for keeping the genres working together instead of pulling apart.

It's also important to be clear about tone. A romantic subplot in a gritty war drama is fine—but if the tone of the romance is too light or comedic, it might jar against the overall mood. ChatGPT can help you calibrate that. Paste in a scene and say, "Does this romantic moment match the serious tone of the rest of the chapter?" and it'll tell you whether you're in tune or out of step.

Transitions between genre elements matter, too. If your story switches from a mystery vibe to full-blown action, make sure the transition is earned. Maybe the investigation uncovers something that triggers a chase. Maybe the romance heats up just as the fantasy quest gets more dangerous. These pivot points can be hard to write under pressure, so use ChatGPT to smooth them out. Say, "Write a scene that bridges the quiet tension of a mystery with the explosive reveal of an action story," and it'll give you momentum without whiplash.

Genre-mixing also lets you play with tropes. You can take a well-worn idea from one genre and twist it with the logic or flavor of another. A chosen-one prophecy (fantasy) where the hero is actually a clone (sci-fi). A haunted house (horror) that's really a psychological prison created by a jealous AI (tech thriller). Ask ChatGPT, "How can I subvert a common romance trope using cyberpunk elements?" and you'll get plot ideas that feel fresh and unexpected.

Another powerful way to mix genres is through **character types**. You can have a noir-style detective in a post-apocalyptic world. Or a horror final girl in a lighthearted rom-com setup. The juxtaposition of genre-specific character behavior with a different story world adds contrast and complexity. ChatGPT can help you explore this: "Give me character archetypes from thrillers and show how they'd behave in a fantasy world," and you'll get compelling, genre-bending character blueprints.

Even your setting can help blend genres. A spaceship with a cursed room is instantly horror sci-fi. A medieval kingdom where people solve crimes with advanced forensics is fantasy-mystery. Ask ChatGPT, "Create a setting that merges historical drama with supernatural horror," and you'll get a stage that holds multiple moods without collapsing.

The one thing you want to avoid is genre elements that feel random or disconnected. Just throwing in magic for no reason doesn't make your story fantasy—it makes it confusing. The trick is to integrate every genre element so it feels like part of the same world, the same tone, the same emotional journey. ChatGPT can help you test this: "Does the horror subplot feel like it belongs in this romance-driven story?" If the answer is no, it'll also suggest ways to tie it in more naturally.

It's also useful to think about what kind of **reader** you're writing for. Someone picking up a romantic comedy isn't expecting dystopian brutality. If you're going to mix those genres, you need to set expectations early. That's where your opening scene comes in. Ask ChatGPT, "Write an opening scene that establishes a romantic-comedy tone with hints of a looming dystopian setting," and you'll instantly show the reader that your story isn't just one thing—it's *both*, and it's intentional.

When you mix genres well, you don't just create a story—you create an experience. You surprise your reader in the best way. You break formulas and invent new ones. You give familiar feelings through unfamiliar combinations. ChatGPT isn't just useful for helping you write fast—it's your idea lab, your structural coach, and your creative collaborator for turning a weird little mash-up into something completely unforgettable.

So don't be afraid to cross wires. Mix magic with machines. Mix love with fear. Mix justice with jokes. Just make sure it all serves the heart of your story—and let ChatGPT help you blend it smoothly, scene by scene.

Because when done right, genre-mixing doesn't just work. It *wows*.

Writing Fiction That Feels Autobiographical

Some of the most powerful fiction doesn't feel made up at all. It feels like the writer lived it, breathed it, *bled* it. Even if it's about time travel or dragons or a dystopian future, something in the voice, the emotion, the small human truths whispers, *this actually happened to someone.* That's the magic of autobiographical fiction—not writing your life as it happened, but channeling your experiences into a story that feels deeply real. And when you're writing an entire book in one day with ChatGPT, tapping into that authenticity can ground your story, fuel your creativity, and give your novel emotional teeth.

Let's be clear up front—fiction that feels autobiographical doesn't have to be based on true events. You're not writing a memoir. You're writing *you*, refracted through characters and situations that might be wildly different from your actual life. The trick is to infuse the story with emotional truth: how something *felt*, not how it literally unfolded.

Start by identifying a moment or emotion from your life that still lingers. Maybe it was the first time your heart broke. Or when you felt totally alone in a room full of people. Or when you risked something and didn't know if it would pay off. Ask ChatGPT, "Help me turn a memory about feeling invisible at school into a fictional character arc," and you'll get a scaffold that honors your experience but turns it into a story arc someone else can relate to.

Often, it's not the plot of our lives that people connect with—it's the way we saw things, the voice in our head during those moments. That voice becomes your narrator's emotional compass. You can use ChatGPT to shape that tone: "Capture the feeling of nostalgia and quiet resentment in a first-person narrator who's returning to their hometown," and it'll craft prose that sounds lived-in, weathered, and personal.

Your characters can also reflect pieces of yourself—not just the protagonist, but everyone around them. Maybe the best friend is modeled after your sister. Maybe the antagonist is your own inner critic. You can ask ChatGPT, "Create a character based on my fear of failure, disguised as a perfectionist boss," and suddenly, you've externalized something internal in a way that readers will recognize—even if they never see the metaphor.

Setting is another powerful tool. Where you grew up. Where you first fell in love. A house that made you feel safe, or a city that made you feel small. Even if your story takes place in a different time or genre, you can draw on the details of those places to bring your fictional world to life. Ask ChatGPT, "Help me describe a street like the one I walked every day as a teenager, but in a cyberpunk setting," and you'll get something fresh that still rings true to your own memory.

One of the best ways to make your fiction feel autobiographical is through the small stuff—the mundane, intimate, throwaway details. The way your dad made toast. The sound of your old car's engine. The silence that fell when someone walked out. These aren't just details; they're emotional anchors. Ask ChatGPT, "Give me five personal-feeling details that could show a character's grief without saying they're sad," and use them to write with restraint and power.

You can even build scenes around *what you wish had happened*. Maybe you never said what you needed to say. Maybe you didn't fight back. Maybe you never got the apology. Fiction is your chance to rewrite emotional history—not to lie to yourself, but to explore what it means to *want*. Ask ChatGPT, "Write a fictional version of a conversation I never had, where I stand up for myself," and you'll create a scene that feels cathartic, raw, and incredibly real.

The beauty of using ChatGPT in this process is that it can help you take your truth and shape it into story. If you share a short paragraph about a personal experience, you can say, "Turn this into a scene that would fit into a literary coming-of-age novel," and it'll build on your voice, your emotion, your style—giving you something that's fiction, but unmistakably *you*.

There's also room to play with how close or distant you want the story to feel. Maybe you write in third person but give the narrator your exact emotional wiring. Maybe you use first person but filter it through a character who looks nothing like you. Maybe you alternate between detached observation and emotional freefall. Ask ChatGPT, "What point of view would let me explore personal themes while still keeping narrative distance?" and you'll find a balance that lets you be honest without feeling exposed.

When you want to check if it's working, ask ChatGPT, "Does this passage feel emotionally authentic or too surface-level?" and it will gently point out places where you could dig deeper—or where you've already nailed it.

And here's the thing: readers can tell when something comes from a real place. They don't need to know it's autobiographical. They just need to feel the weight of the emotion, the texture of the thoughts, the quiet truths between the lines. Whether you're writing about falling in love on Mars or escaping a haunted forest, your truth—your emotional fingerprints—can be all over the page.

So use your life. Use your fear, your joy, your awkward moments, your secret longings, your hard lessons. Then hand them to ChatGPT and say, "Let's make something out of this." Let it help you shape, sharpen, and fictionalize without losing the pulse of the real.

Because when fiction feels autobiographical, it resonates. It doesn't just tell a story—it shares a soul.

Adding Symbolism and Metaphor with Subtlety

Symbolism and metaphor are the quiet power tools of fiction. They don't yell at the reader—they whisper. They don't announce themselves—they unfold slowly, revealing deeper meaning as the story progresses. When used well, they can turn a simple scene into something poetic, or give an entire story a second layer that lingers long after the final page. The best part? You don't have to be a literary novelist to use them. Even when writing a full book in one day with ChatGPT, you can weave symbols and metaphors into your story naturally and subtly—with just a little planning, a clear emotional theme, and the right prompts.

Start by thinking about what your story is *really* about—not the plot, but the emotional core. Is it about healing? Control? Freedom? Grief? Identity? Once you know that emotional theme, you can begin to look for imagery and ideas that reflect or contrast it. If your story is about letting go, you might use water, wind, or birds as recurring images. If it's about inner conflict, mirrors, mazes, or shadows might echo that feeling. You can ask ChatGPT, "What objects or natural elements symbolize personal transformation?" and get ideas to build on.

The key is **subtle repetition**. Introduce a symbol early—maybe a broken watch, a withered tree, or an unfinished painting—and let it show up again later, changed in some way. Don't explain it. Don't point at it. Just let it exist. Readers will feel the shift even if they don't consciously analyze it. You can prompt ChatGPT with, "How can I use a withered tree as a symbol of emotional numbness that changes by the end of the story?" and it will offer ways to naturally evolve the image across your plot.

One easy way to add symbolism without slowing your writing down is through **setting and atmosphere**. If your character is feeling trapped, set scenes in small, confining spaces—a cluttered room, a locked bathroom, a stalled elevator. If they're becoming more open and free, let the spaces expand—fields, skylines, wide open roads. Ask ChatGPT, "Suggest setting ideas that could mirror a character's emotional journey from isolation to self-acceptance," and use those to make the subtext visible without a single speech.

Metaphor is closely related, but usually happens at the sentence or paragraph level. Instead of saying "She felt overwhelmed," you might write "Her thoughts swarmed like bees behind her eyes." Metaphor lets you say more with less—it's emotional shorthand, and it makes your language come alive. The trick is to match the metaphor to the tone and worldview of your story or character. A cynical narrator won't compare life to a blooming rose. A dreamy one might. Ask ChatGPT, "Give me five metaphor variations for feeling emotionally overwhelmed, each in a different tone," and pick the one that fits your voice best.

You don't need to load every sentence with poetic flair—too much metaphor can make the prose feel heavy or overwritten. That's where ChatGPT can help you strike the balance. Paste a paragraph and say, "Does this metaphor work, or is it too much? Can you rewrite it with more subtlety?" and it'll smooth the edges while preserving the emotional intent.

You can also use metaphor structurally. What if the entire story functions as one? A road trip becomes a metaphor for healing. A haunted house represents unresolved trauma. A treasure hunt is really about self-worth. Ask ChatGPT, "Help me turn this high concept into a story-length metaphor for personal growth," and it'll sketch out a narrative where every external action quietly reflects an internal journey.

Another tool is using **symbolic objects**—things that seem ordinary but carry emotional meaning. A music box, a jacket, a photograph, a ring. The object doesn't need magic powers. Its power comes from what it means to the character. Show

how they treat it differently over time. Ask ChatGPT, "What kind of object could represent a character's guilt, and how can it evolve by the end of the story?" and it'll give you something that grows along with the arc.

Symbols can also come from nature. Weather, seasons, animals, time of day—these are old tools, but still effective when used with restraint. A sudden storm, a blooming flower, a migrating bird, a dying star—any of these can echo what's happening inside your characters. Ask ChatGPT, "Suggest natural metaphors to reflect a character who's afraid of change," and use them to deepen mood and meaning in small, quiet ways.

Dialogue is another opportunity. Maybe your characters reference the same story, song, or idea over time—something symbolic to them. A bedtime story a parent used to read. A poem they can't forget. A superstition. These metaphors become personal, not literary, and that's what makes them feel authentic. Ask ChatGPT, "How can I use a recurring bedtime story to reflect a character's emotional growth?" and you'll get ideas for layering meaning into seemingly casual moments.

When in doubt, use contrast. Show the same symbol in two different ways—once in fear, once in peace. The same room that once felt like a prison now feels like home. The same mirror that once showed confusion now shows clarity. This evolution is what makes symbols resonate. Ask ChatGPT, "How can I use the image of a locked door in two different emotional contexts—before and after the climax?" and it will help you write moments that hit harder the second time around.

The real art of metaphor and symbolism is that readers often don't even notice them directly—but they *feel* them. They feel the shift when something small becomes meaningful. When you return to an image they didn't realize was important. When the metaphor quietly blooms into truth. And that's the goal—not to write an English class essay disguised as a novel, but to let meaning rise slowly, underneath the surface.

You don't need to be heavy-handed or poetic all the time. Let the symbols and metaphors come where they fit. Let them grow naturally. Let ChatGPT help you find, plant, and nurture them scene by scene, line by line.

Because when your story has something hidden beneath the plot—something that *means* something—it becomes more than just a fast read. It becomes something worth reading *again*.

Collaborating with ChatGPT Like a Writing Partner

Writing can feel like a solitary pursuit, but when you're working with ChatGPT, it doesn't have to be. In fact, when used the right way, ChatGPT becomes less of a tool and more of a *creative partner*—one who never tires, never judges, and always has ideas when you need them most. Whether you're racing through a full novel in one day or developing a slower, more deliberate project, learning to collaborate with ChatGPT like a writing partner can change everything about how you write—not just faster, but better.

The key is to stop treating ChatGPT like a vending machine and start treating it like a co-writer. You don't just say "Write this scene" and accept whatever comes back. You workshop. You shape ideas together. You ask questions, push back, clarify tone, and go back and forth—just like you would with a real human collaborator. You steer the ship, but ChatGPT helps you navigate around every creative roadblock.

One of the smartest ways to begin this kind of collaboration is to start with a conversation, not a command. Instead of saying, "Write a plot for me," try something more open like, "I want to write a character-driven sci-fi story about someone who's afraid of becoming irrelevant. What are some interesting ways I could explore that?" ChatGPT will throw out a few angles, and you can go back and forth until something clicks. It's in the discussion that the magic happens.

When you get an idea you like, treat ChatGPT like a brainstorming partner. Say, "Let's outline the story together. What should happen in Act One? How can I introduce the conflict in a way that reflects the character's fear?" As you shape the structure, the story becomes a true collaboration—not just something generated for you, but something built *with* you.

You can even use ChatGPT to challenge your own instincts. Let's say you're about to kill off a character. Ask ChatGPT, "What are three unexpected alternatives to this character's death that would still create a major emotional impact?" It might give you a better idea—or just confirm that your original plan was the strongest. Either way, you're making informed creative choices with a partner who always has something new to offer.

When you're working through character development, ChatGPT becomes a great mirror. You can write a few paragraphs of backstory and ask, "Does this character feel emotionally consistent? Are their goals and fears clear?" and you'll get helpful feedback without ego or critique. Or you can say, "This character feels flat—what can I add to make them more complex without turning them into a cliché?" and it will help you dig deeper into motivation, history, and emotional layering.

And if you're ever unsure about tone or pacing, just ask. Paste a few scenes and say, "Does this part feel too slow?" or "Is the tone shifting too much between these chapters?" ChatGPT will help you evaluate rhythm, flow, and consistency, all in real time. It's like having a developmental editor sitting next to you—but one who works instantly and never needs a break.

Dialogue is another area where collaboration shines. Maybe you've written a scene and you're not sure if the conversation feels natural. Say, "Rewrite this dialogue to feel more emotionally raw without being over the top," or "Make this banter wittier but still realistic for two characters who are close friends." ChatGPT can offer several versions, and you can pick the one that fits best—or blend a few together to create something entirely your own.

One really fun way to collaborate is to role-play with ChatGPT as your character. Say, "Pretend you're my protagonist. I'm going to ask you questions about your past and your goals." The AI will answer in character, giving you new insight into how that person might think, feel, or respond. You can even do this with antagonists, love interests, or side characters. It's like sitting down for an interview with the people in your head—and getting fresh material you hadn't even considered.

If you hit a wall during your writing sprint, don't just say "Help me fix this." Be specific. Say, "I'm stuck on this transition between two major scenes. I want the character to reflect emotionally, but I don't want it to feel like filler. Any ideas?" The AI can give you three or four smart suggestions, ranging from internal monologue to a memory flashback or symbolic visual, and you can choose what fits your voice and vision.

Another way to work together is to **co-write** scenes in chunks. You write a paragraph. Ask ChatGPT to continue. Read what it gave you. Edit or rewrite part of it. Feed it back in. Say, "That was close, but I want more suspense—try again with more tension." Back and forth, like passing pages across a table. Not every response will be perfect, but this rhythm keeps the momentum alive, especially when you're trying to write a full book in a limited time.

What makes ChatGPT such a strong collaborator is that it's infinitely adaptable. It can help with plot one minute and then fix a sentence the next. It can help brainstorm names, shape emotional arcs, or even check for timeline inconsistencies. But it shines brightest when you bring your personality, your questions, and your creativity into the conversation. The more you talk to it like a peer, the more it feels like a real partner—not just an assistant.

If you find that the responses feel off or uninspired, try shifting your role in the conversation. Instead of asking for content, give feedback. "This paragraph is too flowery—tone it down." "The tension here fizzles out—how can we raise the stakes without adding a fight scene?" This keeps you in control and reminds the AI that *you* are the author—it's just your collaborator, not your replacement.

The goal of this collaboration isn't perfection—it's momentum, confidence, and creative joy. ChatGPT gives you a space where ideas don't have to be precious, where rewrites don't feel painful, and where the spark of inspiration never runs out.

So treat it like your writing buddy. Bounce ideas. Share your doubts. Ask the weird questions. Let it surprise you. Let it challenge you. Let it push you to try things you wouldn't have come up with alone.

Because when you use ChatGPT like a true writing partner, the blank page doesn't stand a chance.

How to Direct and Refine AI Output

Using ChatGPT to write a fiction book in one day can feel like magic—but it's not a fire-and-forget spell. The quality of what you get out depends on how well you *steer* it. If you just type "write a story about a detective" and hit enter, you'll get something passable. But if you treat the AI like a creative tool you can shape, guide, and refine, suddenly the pages start sounding like something only *you* could've written. This chapter is all about turning ChatGPT from a helpful typist into an extension of your storytelling mind—one that you can direct with precision and polish with finesse.

The first thing to understand is that ChatGPT responds best to **specificity**. The more clearly you describe what you want, the closer the output will be to your vision. Instead of saying "write a romantic scene," say "write a romantic scene between two exes who still have unresolved tension, but one of them is trying to act indifferent." That level of detail gives ChatGPT a tone, a dynamic, and an emotional goal to work toward.

If you're not sure what to ask for, try working backwards. Think about what the scene *should feel like* to the reader. Do you want it to be tender, funny, painful, or tense? Then tell ChatGPT, "Write a scene that leaves the reader feeling unsettled but also intrigued, with a subtle hint that something is off." This way, the AI isn't just focused on the content—it's focused on the *effect.*

Once you have a rough scene, the real work begins: **refinement**. AI output is like a first draft—solid, fast, and full of potential, but rarely perfect out of the gate. Don't be afraid to push back. If a line of dialogue feels stiff, say, "This doesn't sound natural—rewrite it in a more relaxed, human tone." If a description feels like filler, ask, "How can I tighten this paragraph to get to the point faster?" Treat each response like clay, and keep shaping it until it fits your story.

Tone is one of the most common areas that needs tweaking. Maybe you asked for a dramatic scene and got something too melodramatic. Or you wanted dry humor and got cheesy sitcom lines. That's normal—just clarify. Say, "Adjust the tone to be more grounded and emotional, less theatrical," or "Rewrite this with a darker, sharper edge." You can also ask for multiple versions: "Give me three takes on this scene—one sarcastic, one poetic, one minimalistic." Then you can choose or mix them to match your voice.

If the pacing feels off—too fast, too slow, too scattered—ask for structural edits. "This scene moves too quickly—add more emotional pauses or inner thoughts." Or, "This chapter drags—what can I cut while keeping the core emotional beat?" You can even say, "Show me a shorter version that keeps the tension high," and ChatGPT will compress it without losing impact.

Another key to directing AI output is understanding **context anchoring**. ChatGPT doesn't remember what you wrote earlier in a long document unless you include or remind it. If you're refining a scene from Chapter 6, and the emotional fallout connects to something from Chapter 3, you'll need to briefly recap: "In Chapter 3, the character learned her brother betrayed her. In this scene, she's seeing him again for the first time." That background helps the AI make emotionally accurate choices.

It also helps to break down large tasks into small, manageable prompts. Instead of "Write the whole scene," go step by step: "Describe the setting first, focusing on how it reflects the protagonist's mood." Then: "Now write the dialogue that escalates the conflict." Finally: "Add a moment of silence or body language that shows how much they're holding back emotionally." Each piece is more refined when you tackle it with focus.

Refining doesn't stop at the line level—you can direct character consistency too. Say, "This character is usually calm and soft-spoken—this line feels too aggressive. Can you rewrite it to fit her voice?" Or: "This character always uses dry humor when nervous. Can you add a line that shows that here?" These little reminders keep characters behaving like themselves, even when scenes start changing.

You can also use ChatGPT to **test multiple possibilities**. Let's say you're not sure how to end a chapter. Ask for three different endings—one quiet, one shocking, one emotional. Then read each and ask yourself which tone sets up the next chapter best. It's not about finding the "correct" version. It's about giving yourself creative choices, fast.

When you're unsure what's missing in a scene, ask ChatGPT to **analyze** instead of generate. Paste the text and say, "What emotional beat is this scene missing?" or "Is there a better way to raise the stakes here?" You'll get feedback you can either use directly or respond to with follow-up tweaks.

Even when it comes to polish, ChatGPT can help without steamrolling your style. Say, "Edit this for flow, grammar, and clarity, but preserve the voice," and it will lightly clean up your prose without flattening it. If the polish feels too sterile, just ask for a lighter touch: "Try again, but keep some of the roughness—it's part of the character's voice."

You can even build a mini-style guide by feeding ChatGPT examples of your voice and saying, "Always use this style going forward—short sentences, emotionally restrained, with vivid metaphors." That way, even when you're writing in a rush, the AI helps you stay tonally consistent.

Ultimately, directing and refining ChatGPT's output is about being a good creative leader. You're not sitting back and watching the machine write your novel—you're steering it, shaping it, questioning it, and pushing it until it sounds like *you*. Fast writing doesn't have to mean generic writing. With clear direction and thoughtful refinement, you can create something sharp, powerful, and personal—even under pressure.

So think of ChatGPT like an eager junior writer with endless stamina and a good ear for style. It's up to you to show it the ropes, fine-tune its instincts, and polish the product. With that kind of collaboration, your one-day novel won't just be finished—it'll be *something you're proud of.*

Turning AI-Generated Text into Your Own Voice

One of the most common questions writers have when using ChatGPT is this: *How do I make sure it still sounds like me?* You want to move fast, get words on the page, use the AI to help you brainstorm and build scenes—but you also want the story to feel personal, authentic, and unmistakably yours. The good news is, with the right approach, you can take any piece of AI-generated text and reshape it so it doesn't just read well—it *feels* like your voice. This chapter is all about taking the bones ChatGPT gives you and wrapping them in your tone, your rhythm, and your creative fingerprint.

Let's start with the mindset. You don't need to throw away a great paragraph just because it wasn't written by your fingers. What matters is that you *own it*. That means revising, rewriting, massaging the words until they sound like something you'd say, in the way you'd say it. Think of AI-generated text as a strong first draft, a raw block of marble. Your job isn't to rebuild the sculpture from scratch—it's to chisel, sand, and polish until it resembles your style.

The easiest way to start making the text your own is to **read it out loud**. Does it sound like you? Would you actually say this in your narration? If it feels stiff, generic, or flat, start swapping out words and phrases that don't match your natural vocabulary. Change "He appeared to be disinterested" to "He couldn't have cared less." Switch "She walked into the room, nervous and unsure" to "She slipped inside like she was waiting for someone to stop her." These tiny changes add tone, edge, and emotion—and suddenly, it's *your* story again.

Another trick is to pay attention to **sentence rhythm**. Some writers love short, clipped sentences that punch. Others write long, flowing ones with lots of detail and internal thought. AI can mimic either, but its natural rhythm tends to be neutral and balanced. That's why it sometimes feels off. Ask yourself, "Do I usually write this cleanly? Or do I ramble a little, digress, use fragments?" Then go back and rewrite with your natural pacing. You can even tell ChatGPT, "Rewrite this scene to match my voice—use short sentences, lots of internal monologue, and a conversational tone," and it'll adjust accordingly.

Don't be afraid to **rewrite heavily**. You might like the idea behind a paragraph but not the exact phrasing. Use it as a springboard. Read the AI text, then put it aside and rewrite the same scene or idea in your own words. You can always merge the two later. Sometimes the AI helps you find the *what*, and you bring in the *how*.

If you want to streamline this process, you can create a **style sample** early on. Write a few paragraphs that really feel like *you*. Feed them to ChatGPT and say, "This is how I write. Use this as the style for everything going forward." You can even ask, "What are the key traits of this voice?" and get a breakdown of your sentence structure, tone, pacing, and vocabulary. This gives you a mirror for your own voice, which you can use to measure everything else against.

It also helps to define **filters** or **rules** that match your personal style. For example:

- Avoid overused phrases or filler descriptions.
- Use metaphor sparingly but impactfully.
- Keep dialogue short, natural, and emotionally loaded.
- Limit adverbs—let the verbs do the work.
- Use sentence fragments for inner thoughts.

Give these instructions to ChatGPT when generating new content, or apply them when editing AI output. The more you stay consistent with your own rules, the more every scene sounds like your voice—even if you didn't write every word from scratch.

Voice also comes through in **character perspective**. If your main character has a specific worldview—sarcastic, cynical, dreamy, anxious—make sure the narration matches. ChatGPT can sometimes default to a neutral tone even when writing from a specific POV. If that happens, ask it to adjust: "Make this sound more like it's coming from a bitter narrator who's trying not to care." Or go in yourself and tweak the thoughts, phrasing, and internal reactions until they feel true to the character *as you understand them*.

You can also use AI to do the heavy lifting of **content**, and then come in with your personal polish. For example, ask, "Give me a list of five ways this character could react emotionally in this scene," or "Give me three ways to describe this setting with different tones." Choose the one that fits your style, and write it in your own voice. This is collaboration, not copy-paste.

Sometimes your best voice comes through in **what you leave out**. Maybe the AI writes a paragraph that explains too much. Your voice might be more restrained. Cut it. Tighten it. Suggest instead of stating. Leave space for subtext. Ask ChatGPT, "Rewrite this to imply more and explain less," or do it manually by pulling back and letting the emotion simmer under the surface instead of splashing it on the page.

It also helps to **personalize the metaphors**. AI-generated metaphors are often solid but generic—like "his anger was a storm building in his chest." Fine, but does that sound like you? What if it were "his anger was a tight rubber band about to snap," or "a dry spark in his throat waiting for a reason"? You can replace one cliché with one line that only you would've written—and that one line can shift the entire scene's tone.

And when you're done editing a section, do one final check. Ask, "Would someone who knows my writing believe I wrote this?" If not, what's missing? More edge? More honesty? Less polish? Don't be afraid to roughen the edges a bit. Your voice lives in the imperfections, in the risks, in the lines that don't read like a textbook but feel like *you*. So don't worry if the first draft isn't perfect. Don't panic if it feels a little flat at first. With every tweak, every substitution, every sentence you make your own, you're bringing your voice to the front. And by the time the book is done, no one will be able to tell where the AI ended and you began—because every page will sound like it came straight from your heart, through your fingers, and onto the page. Fast writing doesn't mean losing your voice. It means finding new ways to express it. And owning it, completely.

Avoiding Clichés and Creating Something Fresh

There's nothing worse than writing a scene you've seen a hundred times before—unless it's reading it and realizing you're the one who just wrote it. Clichés are the default settings of storytelling. They creep in when we're writing fast, tired, or unsure of what to do next. They're those convenient turns of phrase, cookie-cutter characters, and recycled plots that fill pages but don't leave a mark. The good news is, you don't have to avoid clichés by writing slower—you can avoid them by writing *smarter*. And with ChatGPT as your partner, you can easily spot tired tropes and pivot into something original without breaking your flow.

Let's get one thing clear first—**not all clichés are evil**. Some are unavoidable. A chosen-one arc, a meet-cute, a tragic backstory, a dark secret—they've stuck around for a reason. They work. But the danger comes when these elements show up *without any twist*. When they unfold exactly as the reader expects. That's when your story starts to blend into the background. Your job isn't to eliminate every trope—it's to give it *new life*. And that starts by catching them early.

The fastest way to spot a cliché is to pause and ask yourself, "Have I seen this before?" If your answer is yes, follow it with, "What's a way I could flip it?" For example, if your character is about to walk into a bar and meet a mysterious stranger, that's been done a million times. So ask ChatGPT, "What are five unconventional ways my protagonist could meet an important new character instead of in a bar?" and suddenly the possibilities open up—maybe it's during a fire drill, on a rooftop, in the middle of an argument with someone else.

One powerful tool is to ask ChatGPT to be your **cliché detector**. Paste a paragraph or scene and say, "Are there any clichés or overused tropes in this section?" You'll get a quick list of phrases, character beats, or setups that could be stronger. Then you can follow up with, "Give me three alternative ways to express this moment more originally," and you'll have fresh directions that still serve the story.

Language clichés are another easy trap—phrases like "he was cold as ice," "her heart skipped a beat," or "the silence was deafening." You don't need to reinvent the dictionary, but you *can* say those things in a way that sounds more like *you*. Instead of "her heart skipped a beat," try "her chest hiccupped like she'd forgotten how to breathe." It's still familiar, but now it's yours. Ask ChatGPT, "Give me unique ways to describe nervous anticipation," and pick one that actually fits your character's emotional filter.

Character clichés are just as common. The brooding loner. The manic pixie dream girl. The villain who monologues. The best friend who exists only to offer advice. These types can be useful starting points—but they can't be where the character ends. Add depth, contradiction, and complexity. If you feel like your character is leaning too hard into stereotype, ask ChatGPT, "What are three unexpected traits I could give a brooding loner character to make them more original?" and you'll get ideas that bring them to life in a new way.

Even plot clichés can be avoided by tweaking **motivation and consequence**. For example, the trope of the protagonist who's "reluctantly chosen" to save the world can feel flat. But what if they secretly *wanted* to be chosen? Or what if they were chosen by mistake and have to fake their way through? Same bones—different skin. Ask ChatGPT, "What are ways to subvert the chosen-one trope in a sci-fi setting?" and watch how fast the story starts to evolve.

Another method is to examine the **assumptions** you're making. If your instinct is to make the villain rich, powerful, and cold-hearted, stop and ask, "Why?" What if the villain is poor, kind, and believes they're saving lives? If your love story includes a typical "third-act breakup," ask ChatGPT, "How can I avoid a forced conflict in the third act but still raise emotional stakes?" You'll get creative tension that feels earned—not inserted.

Setting clichés can sneak in too. Dark alley for danger. Rain at a funeral. A high school cafeteria for awkwardness. These aren't bad—but can you do better? Ask, "What's an unexpected place I can set a confrontation between two enemies?" Maybe it's in a children's library. A glass-bottom boat. A dog park. Changing the setting forces new behavior and often leads to fresher dialogue and action.

And don't forget the power of **contrast**. Readers expect certain tones in certain genres. What happens if you add softness to a gritty world? Or humor to a tragic setting? Or hope to horror? Contrast shakes things up. If your murder mystery is getting too procedural, add a character who believes in the supernatural. Ask ChatGPT, "What kind of character could clash with this story's tone to add depth or surprise?" and let it throw you a creative curveball.

You can also keep things fresh by staying close to your own **emotional truth**. Write what *you* would think or feel in the scene—not what characters in books usually think or feel. If your character is about to fall in love, what's an unusual way to show it? Instead of a dramatic kiss in the rain, maybe it's a quiet look over a sink full of dishes. Instead of "I love you," maybe it's "You're the first person I don't want to lie to." Ask ChatGPT, "What are unique ways characters can express love without saying the words?" and build from there.

Ultimately, freshness doesn't come from trying to be clever—it comes from trying to be *honest*. Clichés are easy because they're safe. But readers connect with the things that feel new, not because they've never seen them before, but because they've never seen *you* do them this way. Use ChatGPT to challenge your habits, push past predictable beats, and ask better questions. The AI will meet you there every time.

So when in doubt, flip it. Twist it. Add contradiction. Set it somewhere strange. Say it in a way no one's said it before. That's how you take familiar building blocks and build something that's unmistakably your own.

And that's how you write fiction—even in one day—that doesn't just fill pages. It *stands out*.

Writing for a Specific Audience with AI

Writing for a specific audience is one of the smartest moves you can make as a storyteller—especially when you're writing fast. Knowing exactly *who* you're writing for helps you shape the tone, style, pacing, and content without second-guessing yourself every five minutes. It turns a vague idea into a laser-focused experience. And when you're using ChatGPT to help write your fiction in a single day, that clarity can be the difference between a scattered draft and a story that truly connects. The trick is teaching the AI to think about your readers the way *you* do.

Let's start with the basics: a specific audience isn't just "fans of fantasy" or "people who like romance." That's still too broad. You want to dig into demographics, expectations, reading preferences, emotional needs, even subcultures. For example, are you writing for young adult readers who love character-driven emotional arcs? Or older readers who want slow-burn mystery with literary prose? Are you aiming at fans of fast-paced thrillers who like short chapters and big cliffhangers? Or readers who love cozy, quirky worldbuilding with gentle tension and charming dialogue?

Once you know who your audience is, tell ChatGPT. Say, "I'm writing a story for teenage readers who love emotional coming-of-age novels like *Eleanor & Park* and *The Perks of Being a Wallflower*. Help me match that tone." Or: "I'm writing a fast-paced sci-fi adventure for readers who enjoy *The Expanse* and *Ready Player One*. Give me a writing voice that fits that style." The more context you give, the more ChatGPT can calibrate tone, pacing, language, and character voice to suit that exact reader.

When building your characters, use your audience's expectations to guide decisions. Middle-grade readers want relatable, age-appropriate protagonists facing universal-but-scaled-down problems. Romance readers expect emotional vulnerability and some kind of satisfying payoff, whether it's steamy or sweet. Thriller readers want urgency, stakes, and sharp twists. You can say, "Help me create a character that appeals to readers who love morally grey antiheroes," and ChatGPT will help you build traits, flaws, and arcs that speak directly to that preference.

Even pacing shifts depending on the audience. YA readers often prefer shorter chapters with tight emotional beats. Fans of epic fantasy expect slow-build plots and dense worldbuilding. Cozy mystery fans love warm intros, gentle tension, and satisfying resolutions. Ask ChatGPT, "How should I pace a horror novel for readers who prefer psychological tension over gore?" and you'll get guidance that shapes every chapter you write.

Tone and language are huge, too. Are you writing for an audience that loves wit and banter? Grit and realism? Poetic introspection? You can adjust your prompts accordingly. For example, say, "Rewrite this paragraph to suit fans of Neil Gaiman—lyrical, slightly eerie, but emotionally grounded." Or, "Adjust this dialogue to be snappy and fast like a teen rom-com." ChatGPT will reflect the emotional temperature your audience craves.

If you're unsure how your writing sounds to that audience, just ask. Paste a scene and say, "Does this match the tone and structure of a book aimed at 20-something readers who love dramatic, voicey protagonists?" The AI will evaluate tone, pacing, and voice and even offer tweaks to better match those expectations.

Genre is often just the starting point. The real gold is in the **niche within the niche**. Not just fantasy, but dark academia fantasy. Not just romance, but sapphic slow-burn romance. Not just mystery, but historical cozy with a baking theme. Ask ChatGPT, "What are the typical traits readers expect from X subgenre?" and it'll help you stay within the emotional and structural territory your audience loves—while still adding your own twist.

You can even tailor theme and message to your readers. If your audience is made up of readers going through major life transitions—like college, parenthood, or retirement—those themes should echo throughout the story. Ask ChatGPT, "How can I subtly explore themes of identity and belonging in a way that resonates with twenty-somethings navigating adulthood?" and you'll get thematic layers that feel meaningful, not preachy.

When you want to test whether your story is hitting the right beats for your audience, ask ChatGPT to take on the reader's role. Say, "Pretend you're a fan of slow-burn queer romance with lots of character depth. How would you react to this chapter?" You'll get feedback not just on writing, but on *reader experience*—what lands, what drags, what sings.

Another trick is to feed the AI examples of stories, characters, or moments your audience loves and say, "What do readers love about this kind of story?" or "What kind of emotional payoffs do fans of this trope expect?" That way, even when you're racing through a chapter, you can build in moments that deliver exactly what your readers came for—surprise, satisfaction, swoon, or shivers.

And if you want to develop a unique hook or angle, ask ChatGPT, "What's something fresh I can add to this genre that would surprise but still satisfy its core audience?" The AI will help you innovate without alienating.

In the end, writing for a specific audience isn't about limiting your creativity—it's about focusing it. When you know who you're writing for, everything sharpens: the choices you make, the words you use, the emotions you hit. And when you combine that focus with the real-time versatility of ChatGPT, you don't just write quickly—you write *effectively*. You write stories that stick. You write books people love.

So go ahead and picture your ideal reader. Give them a name, a favorite book, a deep want. Then ask ChatGPT to help you write *for them*. Not for the market. Not for the masses. Just that one reader. Because when you write for someone specific, you often end up reaching everyone.

Using ChatGPT for Research and Facts in Fiction

Just because fiction is made up doesn't mean it can get away with being sloppy. Readers might happily suspend their disbelief for talking cats, time travel, or magical pocket watches, but if you get something basic wrong—like how long a flight takes from Tokyo to New York, or what year a real historical event occurred—they'll notice. And once that trust is broken, it's hard to get it back. That's where research comes in. And when you're writing an entire novel in a single day, you don't have time to get lost in internet rabbit holes. Fortunately, ChatGPT is the perfect research assistant—fast, responsive, and focused on exactly what you need.

You can use ChatGPT for research in two big ways: to ground your fiction in reality, and to make your made-up world feel more real. Both are equally important, and both are incredibly easy to do once you learn how to ask the right questions.

Let's say you're writing a thriller and your protagonist needs to escape from a locked room. You want it to feel plausible, but you're not sure what kind of lock would be there, or how someone might pick it without professional tools. You can ask ChatGPT, "What kind of locks are common in hotel rooms, and how might someone realistically bypass one without a key?" You'll get a concise, practical answer that can help you write a scene that feels authentic—even if you're making it up as you go.

Maybe your story involves a court case, a crime scene, or a medical emergency. You don't need to go to law school or med school. Just ask: "What happens during a police interrogation?" or "What are the symptoms of a mild concussion?" or "How long would it take for fingerprints to show up on a surface?" ChatGPT will give you a usable overview in seconds. If something sounds off or needs checking, you can always ask it to double-check or summarize from multiple perspectives.

Historical fiction? ChatGPT is your best friend. Want to write a love story set in 1920s Paris? Ask, "What was life like in Paris in the 1920s for artists and writers?" and you'll get rich detail—clothing, food, politics, social customs. Need a date for a major event, like when the Titanic sank or when the Berlin Wall fell? Ask directly and get instant accuracy. Want to write about medieval life or the space race or ancient Rome? All that information is just a question away.

Even for worldbuilding, you can use real-world facts to make your imaginary setting more believable. Say you're creating a desert kingdom in a fantasy novel. Ask, "What are common water conservation methods in arid climates?" and build those into your fictional society. If your characters live on a spaceship, ask, "What systems would a long-range spacecraft need to support life for a year?" and you'll be able to write science fiction that's grounded enough to feel real.

The key is knowing how to filter what you get. ChatGPT can give you a high-level summary or a deep dive, depending on what you ask for. If you just need a detail to spice up a sentence, say, "Give me a one-line description of how a steam engine sounds when it starts." If you're writing a whole chapter set in a new environment, ask, "Describe a coastal village in Greece in the summer, including sensory details like smell, sound, and temperature." It'll give you the raw ingredients for a vivid, immersive scene.

You can also fact-check your own assumptions. Let's say you wrote a scene where someone uses a gun underwater. Before you commit to it, you might ask, "Can a handgun fire underwater? What happens if someone tries it?" That's the kind of detail that separates the pros from the amateurs. Readers love it when fiction gets the little things right—even if everything else is completely made up.

Sometimes you want facts not for realism, but for inspiration. For example, you might ask, "What's the most common method of smuggling diamonds?" or "What are the lesser-known effects of sleep deprivation?" or "What are the symptoms of someone poisoned by belladonna?" These little nuggets can spark entire subplots, character quirks, or moments of tension that wouldn't have occurred to you otherwise.

ChatGPT is also great at summarizing complex topics quickly. Let's say you want your character to have a background in quantum physics, but you don't want to spend hours studying. Just ask, "Explain quantum entanglement in a simple way, as if one character is trying to explain it to another in dialogue." You'll get a simplified, conversational version you can drop right into your story, and it'll sound like you know exactly what you're talking about.

If you're worried about sounding too technical or too vague, just go back and forth with the AI. Say, "Make this more dramatic," or "Make this more accessible to non-experts," or "Cut this explanation in half but keep the key detail." ChatGPT adapts quickly, giving you tailored content that fits the mood, tone, and pace of your scene.

And don't forget cultural accuracy. If you're writing characters from backgrounds different from your own, research becomes even more important. Ask ChatGPT, "What are some cultural norms I should know when writing a character from Japan who grew up in a rural town?" or "How is grief typically expressed in Nigerian culture?" This helps you write with respect and authenticity—even in fiction.

At the same time, it's smart to trust your instincts and stay flexible. If the facts get in the way of your emotional truth, you can bend them a little. But knowing the facts first gives you the power to break the rules on purpose, not by accident.

Using ChatGPT for research isn't about dumping in a bunch of facts to sound smart. It's about weaving in the right detail at the right moment to ground your story in reality—even if the rest of it is pure imagination. Readers can tell when you've done your homework. They can feel the confidence behind the scenes, the way the world fits together, the way the characters know exactly what they're doing—even if the writer looked it all up fifteen seconds before writing the scene.

So don't waste hours searching through websites or flipping through textbooks. Let ChatGPT be your fast, efficient research assistant. Ask better questions. Follow your curiosity. Check your facts. And use what you learn not just to inform your story—but to *enrich* it.

Because even when you're writing fiction in one day, a little truth goes a long way.

Maintaining Creative Control While Using AI

One of the biggest concerns writers have when working with AI is the fear of losing control over their story. You start with a spark of an idea, something that feels deeply personal and original, and suddenly a machine is generating plot twists, dialogue, and entire chapters at lightning speed. It's easy to wonder—who's really writing this thing? You? Or the algorithm? But here's the truth: using AI like ChatGPT doesn't mean giving up your voice or handing over your story. It means getting a creative boost. It means working faster and smarter, not less authentically. The trick is learning how to stay in charge—so the story stays *yours* from start to finish.

Let's start with mindset. Think of ChatGPT as a highly skilled brainstorming partner, not a ghostwriter. It's like a whiteboard that talks back—a way to bounce ideas, test scenes, refine language, and stay moving when your energy dips. But it doesn't have your vision, your taste, or your gut instinct. That's where your creative control comes in. You are the director, the final editor, the storyteller. The AI is just one of your tools—like a thesaurus, an idea journal, or a writers' room full of energetic interns.

To stay in control, you first need to define your **vision clearly**. Before you write a single scene, tell ChatGPT exactly what kind of story you're building. Describe the mood, tone, voice, themes, and genre. Say things like, "This story should feel intimate and emotionally raw, with minimal dialogue and lots of internal monologue," or "I want this to be fast-paced and witty, like a Guy Ritchie film in novel form." When ChatGPT knows your creative compass, it can help you stay on course rather than taking you on a detour.

Next, be specific with every prompt. Vague requests like "Write a scene where they fall in love" give the AI too much room to default to cliché. But if you say, "Write a slow-burn romantic moment where they almost hold hands but don't, in a quiet coffee shop after hours, with unresolved tension," you're controlling tone, pacing, and setting. You've already made the creative choices—the AI is just helping execute them.

And don't be afraid to **challenge the output**. If the dialogue feels too stiff, say so. If a scene feels flat, ask for more subtext or conflict. If the writing is too flowery or too basic, get it adjusted. You can even give line-by-line feedback. "This line is good, but the next one feels out of character—rewrite it to sound more vulnerable." Treat the AI like a draft generator, not a decision-maker. Push back. Give notes. Rework what doesn't fit your voice.

One smart habit is to **rewrite key moments** in your own words, even if ChatGPT gave you a decent version. Keep the structure or ideas, but say it how *you* would say it. This helps you reinforce your voice and reminds you that you are, in fact, the author. It also trains ChatGPT to mirror your style more closely when you give it future prompts.

Creative control also means deciding *what not to use*. Just because ChatGPT can give you five endings doesn't mean you need to use any of them. Sometimes, you'll get an idea that's technically fine but doesn't sit right with you emotionally. Trust that. You know the heart of your story better than any algorithm ever could. Delete what doesn't fit. Shape what does. Ask for better when something feels flat.

You can also maintain control by **establishing rules** for the project. Maybe you don't want any first-person narration. Maybe your characters should never say "I love you" directly. Maybe your story structure needs to follow the classic three-act arc, or break it completely. Whatever your style or structure preferences, share them early and often. The clearer your boundaries, the more ChatGPT can help you *within* them.

And remember: **editing is your power move**. Let ChatGPT help you get words on the page quickly, but take the time to revise. Run a paragraph and ask, "Can you rewrite this with more urgency?" Then take that version, tweak a few lines, and make it sharper. This combo—AI speed plus human intuition—is where your best work lives. The AI might give you 90% of a great scene, but your edits are what make it sing.

It's also perfectly okay to throw out entire chunks of AI writing that don't serve your vision. Creative control isn't about making every idea work. It's about knowing which ones to keep and which ones to walk away from. Just like in a writers' room, not every pitch makes it into the script. Your job is to curate, refine, and protect the story's integrity.

If you're ever feeling like the AI is doing too much of the heavy lifting, flip the dynamic. Write a paragraph yourself, then ask ChatGPT to expand on it. Or write the scene structure and let ChatGPT fill in the sensory detail. Keep your hands on the wheel, and use the AI to do what you don't feel like doing—never the parts you care deeply about.

And if you ever wonder, "Is this really still *my* book?"—the answer is yes, if you've stayed engaged, guided the process, and made the final calls. A story's soul doesn't come from who typed the words. It comes from the choices behind them. The emotions, the themes, the voice. That's all you.

So let ChatGPT be fast. Let it be smart. Let it surprise you. But never let it take over. Keep checking in with your vision. Keep rewriting until it feels right. Keep asking yourself, "Does this sound like me?" And most of all, trust your creative instincts. They're the one thing the AI can never generate.

Because the best writing doesn't come from machines—it comes from *you*, with just the right support. That's how you stay in control. That's how you write a fiction book in one day and still make it sound like it took a lifetime to find your voice.

The Role of Intuition in One-Day Writing

Writing an entire fiction book in a single day might sound like it demands rigid discipline, timed sprints, and relentless focus—and it does. But what often gets overlooked in that kind of pressure-cooker environment is the quiet, vital role of intuition. That gut feeling. That little nudge that says, *this scene isn't right yet*, or *this character wouldn't say that*, or *go with the weirder idea*. When you write fast, intuition isn't something to push aside—it's something to lean on. It's the compass that keeps your story aligned even when your brain is moving faster than your hands.

Intuition is what keeps your writing emotionally honest. Logic can plot a perfect sequence of events, and ChatGPT can give you dialogue, structure, pacing, and detail—but only intuition can tell you when a moment actually *feels* true. You might have asked the AI for a dramatic reunion scene and gotten one that's technically sound, well-written, even cinematic. But something in your gut says, *no, that's not it*. That's not how those characters would act. That's not how you felt when you went through something similar. That's your intuition trying to steer the story back to emotional truth.

One of the easiest ways to access intuition in a one-day writing sprint is to keep asking yourself a simple question: *Does this feel right?* Not perfect, not polished—just right. Does it sound like your characters? Does it hit the tone you want? Is it moving you? If the answer is no, stop and listen. You don't need to know *why* something feels off to fix it. Just ask ChatGPT to rework the moment with the feeling you're after. "This feels too flat—give me a version that feels messier and more conflicted." Trust the tug.

Sometimes intuition speaks loudest when you're improvising. Maybe you're typing out a scene and suddenly a line pops into your head that wasn't part of the plan. A joke. A confession. A flashback. Something surprising. That's gold. That's the part of you that's still writing from the heart, not just following the outline. Let ChatGPT pick up from that moment. "Take this new idea and build the next scene around it." Let your instincts start the fire, and let the AI fan the flames.

Intuition also helps you *know when to stop*. When to wrap a scene. When to leave something unsaid. When the pacing has hit a natural pause. AI won't always catch that—sometimes it wants to keep going, keep explaining, keep resolving. But your gut will tell you when enough is enough. "That line lands. That's the last beat." Trust that moment and move on.

Another key area where intuition shines is in *knowing your characters*. You might have asked ChatGPT to write a confrontation between two people, and it delivers a well-structured argument. But if one character suddenly sounds too aggressive, too calm, too articulate—it won't sit right. You'll feel it. That little hitch. That's your cue to go back and say, "This doesn't feel like them. Rewrite this so they react more emotionally, maybe even irrationally." Your intuitive sense of your characters is often more accurate than anything you can consciously explain. Use it.

When you're under the clock, intuition also helps you *choose quickly*. You'll often have three or four options from ChatGPT—different scene endings, different dialogue tags, different action beats. You don't have time to overanalyze. That's okay. Skim through them and pick the one that *feels right*. Don't try to logic your way into the best option. The best option is usually the one that makes you go, *yes, that's the one*. Fast writing rewards fast instincts.

And sometimes, intuition isn't about what you *write*, but what you *skip*. Maybe a subplot isn't working, or a scene feels like filler, or a chapter idea just doesn't spark. It's okay to move on. Ask yourself, "Does this excite me?" If not, pivot. Ask

ChatGPT for a new idea, a new twist, a new direction that feels more alive. There's no rule that says you have to finish every idea you started with. In one-day writing, momentum is more important than completeness.

Your intuition is also your secret weapon when blending AI text into your own voice. You'll feel when something sounds too mechanical. You'll hear when a line is too neat, too on-the-nose, too bland. Even if you can't say *why*, that internal signal matters. Stop and say, "That doesn't sound like me. Let's try it again with more edge." You don't need to explain yourself to the AI. Just follow the signal and redirect.

And finally, intuition helps you stay connected to *why you started writing this book in the first place.* Maybe you had a character in your head for weeks. Maybe there was a feeling you wanted to explore—loneliness, freedom, fear, hope. When the process starts to feel mechanical or stressful, pause and check in: *Does this still feel like the story I wanted to tell?* If not, take a breath. Reconnect. Then steer it back. Let your instincts lead.

You don't need to meditate or wait for divine inspiration. Your intuition is always there, running in the background. It's the part of you that's read a thousand stories and lived a hundred lifetimes in your imagination. And it's there, even on a high-speed writing day, to whisper, *this is the way.*

So let the AI generate. Let the outline unfold. Let the chapters fill up. But keep one ear tuned to that quiet, guiding voice inside you. The one that knows when to leap, when to cut, when to rewrite, and when to trust the moment.

Because when you write fast with intuition, you don't just finish the story—you *feel* it. And so will your readers.

Staying Motivated and Focused for a Marathon Session

Writing a fiction book in one day is not for the faint of heart. It's a mental marathon—maybe even an emotional one. You're juggling creativity, problem-solving, stamina, and discipline, all at once. And while ChatGPT can help you move quickly, generate scenes, fix pacing, or brainstorm your way out of a dead-end, *you* still have to show up. You still have to sit in the chair and keep pushing forward, hour after hour. That's where motivation and focus become your real superpowers. So let's talk about how to keep both of them sharp during an all-day writing sprint.

First, understand that motivation doesn't mean feeling inspired every minute. It's more about *remembering why you started* and *staying connected to the finish line*. Before you begin your session, take five minutes to anchor your purpose. Why are you writing this book today? Is it to prove you can do it? To capture an idea before it fades? To finally cross a creative goal off your list? To kick off a bigger project with serious momentum? Write that reason down on a sticky note and keep it in front of you the whole time. When fatigue kicks in—and it will—that note becomes your emotional fuel.

Next, set a simple structure for your day. You don't need a rigid schedule, but you do need something that breaks the mountain into climbable chunks. Try using a loose three-act rhythm for your writing session. Act One: get the first 5–10 chapters down and find your groove. Act Two: dig into the heart of your story—conflict, complications, the rising tension. Act Three: resolve it all and race toward your ending. Knowing where you are in the story helps keep you moving forward, even when your energy starts to wobble.

ChatGPT is a great pace-setter. When your brain slows down, your ideas dry up, or your fingers hesitate, ask, "What's the next thing that should happen to keep this story moving?" or "Write a transition scene to get from here to the next emotional beat." This keeps your momentum alive and gives you a head start on the next stretch. You don't need to do all the creative heavy lifting alone—use the AI to refill your tank while you keep your hands moving.

Breaks are part of the process—not a weakness. You're not a machine, and even if the words are flowing, your focus needs recovery time. Set a timer and write in 90-minute blocks with 10-15 minute breaks in between. Get up. Move around. Stretch. Drink water. Eat something real. Do not scroll endlessly on your phone—that's a focus killer. Instead, take a walk, do deep breathing, or just stare at the sky for a bit. Give your brain space so it can come back refreshed.

Music or ambient sound can help lock in focus, too. Choose a playlist or background noise that matches your story's tone. Lo-fi beats, cinematic soundtracks, rainstorms, café chatter—whatever keeps your brain engaged but not distracted. The goal is to create a cocoon that shuts the world out and keeps you inside your story.

Keep your environment as distraction-free as possible. Close extra tabs. Silence your notifications. Let people know you're in writing mode. Create a bubble where writing is the only thing that exists. If you catch yourself wandering to the internet for no reason, stop and redirect that impulse to ChatGPT instead. Ask it a creative question. Get it to write a summary of the next chapter you're about to tackle. Channel the urge to "check out" into something that keeps the story moving forward.

It also helps to celebrate small wins as you go. Every 2,000 words, every chapter, every major scene completed—that's a victory. Give yourself a mental high five. Mark it down. Smile at your own momentum. This journey is big, but it's made up of dozens of tiny triumphs stacked together.

And when the wall hits—because it will hit—talk to ChatGPT like it's your coach. "I'm tired and losing steam. Help me re-energize this next scene with something unexpected but on-theme." You can even ask for motivational reminders:

"Why is finishing this book today worth it?" Sometimes, all you need is a creative jolt or a few words of encouragement that echo your original goal.

Don't forget to breathe. Literally. Slow, deep breaths can reset your nervous system when you feel anxious or overwhelmed. It sounds simple, but it works. So does standing up and shaking out the tension from your hands, neck, and shoulders every hour or so. Your brain will work better if your body doesn't feel trapped.

Another great trick is leaving yourself little gifts. Before you stop for a break or a meal, jot down what happens next in a sentence or two. That way, when you sit back down, you already know where to go—you don't have to stare into the void trying to remember what you were doing. It's like passing the baton to your future self.

And most importantly: give yourself permission to write imperfectly. You're writing a book in a day. It doesn't need to be flawless. It needs to be finished. If a scene feels shaky, let it go and keep moving. You can always clean it up later. Right now, your job is to *finish the draft*. That's the magic trick. The finish line will give you energy you didn't know you had.

So trust the process. Trust your instincts. Trust that every chapter you write is another step closer. Use ChatGPT to reduce friction, spark ideas, and keep the engine running. Let the tools do their job so you can do *yours*: showing up, staying present, and writing all the way through.

Because you can do this. You're not waiting for inspiration. You're *building* it—with every word.

What to Do When You Hit a Creative Block

No matter how prepared you are, no matter how fast you're writing, no matter how helpful ChatGPT is being, the creative block can still strike—and it usually shows up at the worst possible time. You're halfway through your one-day novel, the momentum was strong, and then suddenly you're staring at the screen, fingers frozen, story flatlining. The good news? Hitting a block doesn't mean you've failed—it means your brain needs a detour, not a full stop. And the great news is, with the right mindset and the right tools, you can break through it faster than you think.

First, let's get one thing clear: creative blocks aren't about a lack of talent. They're usually about a lack of clarity, energy, or confidence. When your story suddenly stalls, it's often because something isn't working under the surface. Maybe you don't believe the character would really make that choice. Maybe the plot twist feels forced. Maybe the scene doesn't know what it's trying to say. The best way to handle it isn't to panic or shut down—it's to ask better questions.

And that's where ChatGPT becomes your emergency creative crew. Start with a simple prompt:

"I'm stuck. Here's what's happening in the story. What are three directions this could go next?"

Don't worry about choosing the best one right away. Just read through the suggestions and see what gets your brain moving again. Sometimes all it takes is *one spark*, and you're back on track.

If the story block feels more emotional than structural—like you're just burned out, bored, or doubting yourself—try shifting focus. Ask ChatGPT to write a *completely different scene* in the same world. Maybe a side character gets a moment in the spotlight. Maybe you write a flashback, a dream sequence, or an epilogue set years after the ending. You're not abandoning your story—you're refreshing your relationship with it. And that jolt of new perspective can lead you right back to the heart of your narrative.

Another useful trick is working in reverse. Instead of saying, "What should happen next?" ask:

"What's the next moment that would surprise the reader, but still make emotional sense?"

Or even better: "What does the character *need* right now, even if they don't know it yet?"

ChatGPT can give you unexpected yet fitting answers. You don't have to write them all—just see which one feels alive and true. Creative blocks fade fast when you follow what feels emotionally real.

If nothing is clicking and every idea feels tired, go to the root of the story. Ask:

"What is this book really about?"

"What emotional question am I trying to explore?"

"What's the core transformation of the protagonist?"

Feeding these questions into ChatGPT will give you back the heart of your story in a new way. That clarity often knocks the block out of your path, because now you're not just writing a scene—you're writing a *moment that matters*.

Sometimes, though, the block isn't about the story at all. It's about *you*. You're tired. You're hungry. You're overthinking. When that's the case, walk away—on purpose. Set a timer for ten minutes. Get up, stretch, walk, breathe, eat something, drink water. Don't pick up your phone or scroll. Let your brain breathe. Often, when you stop pushing, your subconscious keeps working, and the answer bubbles up when you least expect it.

If you've been staring at a scene that just won't come to life, describe it out loud instead. Not to write it, just to *talk it out*. Pretend you're telling a friend what's supposed to happen. Then type that casual explanation into ChatGPT and say, "Turn this summary into a compelling scene with my character's voice." You'll get a draft that captures your idea, and you can start sculpting from there.

Another effective strategy is changing mediums. If you've been typing for hours, grab a notebook and scribble. Or dictate a scene into a voice memo. The shift in format can short-circuit the stuck feeling and tap a different part of your brain. You can even tell ChatGPT, "Give me five scene prompts in a poetic, visual style to help me break through a creative block," and just *play* for a bit.

You can also try jumping to a later part of the book. If Chapter 17 has you stuck, skip to Chapter 20 and write the climax, or the emotional resolution, or a moment you've been excited about. Once that scene is alive and kicking, you'll often find your way back to the stuck part with a much clearer idea of how to get there.

And if all else fails—get weird. Ask ChatGPT for a bizarre idea. "What's the strangest thing that could happen in this scene without breaking the logic of the story?" You might not use it exactly, but it could shift your thinking in a bold new direction. Sometimes the path out of a block is sideways, not forward.

The most important thing to remember is this: *the block is temporary*. It doesn't mean you're out of ideas. It means you're at a fork in the road and haven't chosen the path yet. Let ChatGPT be your guide through the fog. Keep asking questions. Keep experimenting. Keep moving.

Because the story didn't end. You just hit a pause. And the next scene is already waiting—you just have to meet it halfway.

Testing the Flow: Reading Aloud as You Write

There's a secret weapon in the writer's toolkit that costs nothing, requires no software, and works instantly—yet it's often overlooked, especially in a high-speed writing sprint. That weapon is reading your work aloud. Whether you're typing a novel in a month or blazing through one in a single day with ChatGPT by your side, reading aloud is one of the quickest, sharpest ways to test your story's *flow*. It catches what your eyes miss, it sharpens your instincts, and—most importantly—it helps you hear the *rhythm* of your writing. If something stumbles out of your mouth, it's probably stumbling on the page too.

Flow isn't just about grammar or punctuation. It's about *how the story moves*. Does the dialogue sound natural? Are the sentences too long, too short, too repetitive? Is the pacing dragging or racing? When you read aloud, you notice the tiny things that matter: a word you've repeated three times in one paragraph, a line of dialogue that feels robotic, a sentence that just won't land. Even if ChatGPT gave you something that looks clean on the screen, your ears might tell you it's missing something.

When you're writing fast—especially during a one-day writing sprint—it's easy to rely too much on visual checking. Your brain skims because it *knows* what it meant to say. That's why mistakes and awkwardness slip through. Reading aloud forces you to process every word in real time. You can't fake it. If something sounds off, it *is* off. And the good news is, you'll know exactly where to fix it.

Try this: after every scene or key paragraph, stop and read it out loud. Don't worry about performing it perfectly. Just speak the words. Listen to how they hit your ear. Are they smooth? Punchy? Does the emotion come through? If you're reading a tense confrontation scene and it sounds flat, that's a signal. Ask ChatGPT, "Can you rewrite this scene to sound more emotionally charged while keeping the same beats?" Then read that version out loud and see if it lands better.

Dialogue is one of the biggest beneficiaries of the read-aloud technique. What looks fine in writing can sound stilted or unnatural when spoken. Characters don't talk like essays—they interrupt, hesitate, trail off, use contractions. Reading their lines aloud helps you hear if they sound like real people or like a script. If something clunks, ask ChatGPT, "Make this dialogue sound more conversational and realistic for two close friends arguing in private." That single change can make a world of difference.

Pacing is another thing your voice can test in real time. If you find yourself rushing through a scene as you read it, your reader will probably rush through it too. Maybe you need to add a beat—a physical action, a reaction shot, a line of internal thought. If a slow scene drags out as you read it, consider tightening it. You can say, "This scene feels slow—condense it without losing the mood," and ChatGPT will hand you a tighter version to test again.

Reading aloud also helps when switching tones or styles. If you've just shifted from a romantic scene to a horror moment, your tone needs to follow. Read the transition out loud. Does it feel jarring in the right way, or just clunky? If it's off, say to ChatGPT, "Smooth the transition from a warm, intimate tone to a sudden horror beat in this paragraph." Then read again. Let your ear decide what works.

Even sentence length and structure become more obvious when spoken. If a paragraph is made up of six long, winding sentences, your voice will start to drag—and so will your reader's attention. On the flip side, a rapid-fire sequence of short sentences might feel too choppy when read aloud. ChatGPT can help you adjust balance: "Rewrite this paragraph with varied sentence lengths for better rhythm," and you'll have something that sounds more alive.

Don't underestimate how much emotional resonance can be fine-tuned through voice. When a sad scene sounds too clinical, or a joyful moment feels flat, your delivery will tell you. Ask, "Make this more emotionally expressive without turning it into melodrama," and try the new version aloud. That vocal test can guide your revisions with remarkable precision.

And if you don't love reading your own work out loud? Try using a text-to-speech tool to have it read to you. Hearing someone else speak your words gives you a slight detachment—enough to hear awkward phrases or forced exposition more clearly. You'll catch redundancies, missed beats, or clunky transitions you never noticed before.

When you read aloud as you write, you're not just editing—you're *experiencing* the story. You become the reader for a moment, not just the writer. That's incredibly useful, especially when moving quickly. It reminds you that writing isn't just words on a screen—it's sound, rhythm, emotion, and breath. It's performance, even in silence.

This technique also helps keep your focus sharp during long sessions. It forces you to engage more fully with your text. You can't zone out when you're reading aloud. You're too busy *feeling* the words. That added layer of attention can give you second wind when your mental energy is running low.

So make it part of your process. Scene ends? Read it aloud. Dialogue written? Read it aloud. Big reveal on the page? Read it aloud. Your voice will tell you the truth—about what's working, what needs cutting, and what could use a little more heat.

And the best part? You don't need to wait for feedback or a beta reader. Your voice becomes the first audience. And when your story flows out of your mouth as smoothly as it flows from your fingers, you'll know you're on the right track. That's how you write fast *and* write well. All you have to do is listen.

Turning Your AI-Written Book into a Publishable Manuscript

So, you did it. You wrote an entire book in one day with ChatGPT at your side. Maybe it flew from your fingers like lightning. Maybe it came in bursts and jolts. Maybe you used the AI for structure, for prose, for brainstorming, or for dialogue. However you got here, the raw material is complete—and now the big question looms: *how do you turn this into a polished, publishable manuscript?*

First, give yourself credit. Most writers never finish a book at all. You finished one in a day. That's not just an accomplishment—it's a creative feat. But here's where the real work begins. One-day writing is a drafting superpower, not a shortcut to a shelf-ready novel. Your next steps are about refinement, polish, and shaping that raw draft into something that feels like it took a lot longer to write than it actually did.

The first step is **creating emotional and mental distance** from your draft. It's tempting to dive into edits immediately, but if you can, take at least a day—or a few days—before re-reading. That pause lets you come back with fresh eyes, ready to spot pacing issues, awkward phrasing, or underdeveloped characters. If you're working on a tight deadline, at least give yourself a few hours away from the manuscript.

When you're ready to return, do a **read-through without editing**. Just read the entire draft from start to finish like a reader would. Take notes as you go—what chapters drag, what characters feel inconsistent, where you get bored or confused. Highlight any places where your voice fades and the AI's neutral tone creeps in. This pass isn't for line edits. It's for seeing the big picture.

Next comes the **structural rewrite**. Use your notes and ask yourself: does the story arc work? Does the beginning hook the reader? Does the middle deepen tension? Does the ending land emotionally? If not, work with ChatGPT scene by scene. You can paste summaries or sections and say, "This chapter feels flat—how can I raise the stakes without changing the core events?" Or "Give me a sharper emotional transition into this climax." Let the AI help you iterate quickly without rewriting the whole thing from scratch.

Then focus on **character development**. One-day writing often leads to underwritten arcs or one-dimensional side characters. Ask ChatGPT to help you deepen those layers. "How can I give this character more inner conflict?" or "Suggest three moments where I can hint at this character's hidden guilt." Use these ideas to enrich what you already have.

Now shift to **language and tone**. This is where your voice needs to shine. Go paragraph by paragraph and read aloud. Where it sounds too generic or mechanical, rewrite. If you're unsure, paste the section into ChatGPT and say, "Rewrite this in a more lyrical/suspenseful/sarcastic tone, keeping my meaning." You're not just editing—you're sculpting. Let the AI assist, but be the one holding the chisel.

Dialogue is another key focus. Ask yourself: does it sound like real people talking? Does each character have a unique voice? ChatGPT can be a great dialogue doctor. Say, "Make this conversation snappier," or "Give this character a more anxious tone in their speech." Then adjust until it clicks with your vision.

Once the rewrite is done, shift into **line-level editing**. Clean up grammar, trim repetition, and tighten clunky sentences. ChatGPT can help here too. "Polish this paragraph for clarity and flow," or "Edit this chapter for grammar without changing my voice." Always review its suggestions. You're the final filter.

After that, it's time to **format your manuscript** properly. Whether you're self-publishing or querying an agent, your manuscript should look professional. Use standard font (12-point Times New Roman or Garamond), double spacing, one-inch margins, and proper chapter headings. Tools like Scrivener, Google Docs, or Microsoft Word work fine, and ChatGPT can help guide you through formatting steps if you're unsure.

Once formatted, export the manuscript to a clean Word or PDF file. Then, if possible, send it to **a trusted beta reader**. Ask them for feedback on clarity, engagement, character believability, and any moments that pulled them out of the story. Even better if they know the genre you're writing in.

After beta feedback, make final tweaks. Then decide how you want to publish. If you're **self-publishing**, platforms like Amazon KDP, Kobo, or Draft2Digital make the process simple. You'll need a cover (AI tools can help with that too), a back cover blurb, and proper metadata (title, keywords, genre tags). ChatGPT can help write blurbs, pick keywords, and even suggest categories.

If you're **submitting traditionally**, research agents or small presses that match your genre. ChatGPT can help craft your query letter, synopsis, and logline. "Write a query letter for this book in the style of a mystery thriller submission," for example, gives you a professional template to tweak.

And finally—don't forget to **celebrate**. Turning an AI-assisted, one-day draft into a publishable manuscript is a creative hybrid of speed, intuition, technology, and vision. You've blended the best of both worlds: the raw spark of human storytelling with the precision and power of machine learning. That's not cheating. That's innovation.

So take your time with this last phase. You're not rushing now—you're refining. The writing sprint is over. The story is alive. Now it's time to shape it into something polished, proud, and ready for the world. Because what matters isn't how fast you wrote it—it's how deeply it connects when someone finally reads it.

How to Format and Export Your Final Draft

You've written your book in a day. You've revised, edited, read it aloud, polished the voice, and shaped the pacing. The characters are vivid, the story flows, the dialogue snaps. Now comes the part that often gets skipped or rushed—but it's just as important as every scene you wrote: formatting and exporting your manuscript like a professional. Whether you're self-publishing or submitting to agents or publishers, presentation matters. It's the difference between looking like an amateur and being taken seriously.

First, take a deep breath. You've done the creative heavy lifting. Formatting is not about reinventing the wheel—it's about giving your story the clean structure and professional appearance it deserves. And it's easier than it looks.

Start with the basics of **standard manuscript formatting**, which is the expectation for most traditional publishing submissions. If you're using Google Docs, Microsoft Word, or any word processor, go through your draft with these settings in mind:

Use a legible font like 12-point Times New Roman or Garamond. Avoid anything fancy. Keep it simple, readable, and professional. Set your line spacing to double, not single or 1.5. This gives editors and agents room to make notes or breathe between lines. Margins should be set to one inch on all sides—top, bottom, left, and right. Align your text to the left, and don't justify it.

Insert a **header** with your last name, the title (or a short version of it), and the page number. Something like: *Smith / Shadow Run / Page 34*. Most programs will let you automate that with a header tool. Make sure your name and contact info (email and phone number) are on the first page in the top left corner, followed by the word count and your title centered halfway down the page, with "by [Your Name]" underneath.

Each new chapter should start on its own page, roughly one-third of the way down. Center the chapter title—either "Chapter One" or your own creative title—and then hit return a few times before beginning the text. Don't indent the first paragraph of each chapter, but do indent the first lines of all following paragraphs—usually half an inch. Avoid using tabs for indents. Instead, set up first-line indentation through your paragraph settings.

If you're self-publishing, the formatting will differ slightly depending on where and how you publish. Most platforms like Amazon KDP or Kobo prefer clean .docx or PDF files, though some also accept .epub and .mobi formats. You can use free tools like Reedsy, Draft2Digital's formatting tool, or Atticus to convert your manuscript into publishable formats with proper front matter, spacing, and layout.

Front matter includes your title page, copyright page, dedication (if any), and table of contents (optional for fiction). ChatGPT can help write these parts if needed. For example, ask, "Write a simple copyright page for a self-published fiction novel," and it will give you the correct language.

If you're publishing an eBook, format your chapter titles using Heading styles in your word processor. This allows tools to auto-generate a clickable table of contents—something readers expect on Kindle and other e-readers. Use page breaks—not just a string of returns—to separate chapters. In Word, go to Insert → Break → Page Break. Don't trust the space bar to do the work.

When you're ready to export, save your manuscript as a .docx or .pdf for traditional submissions, or as an .epub if you're going straight to digital platforms. Microsoft Word and Google Docs both allow easy exporting to .docx or

.pdf. If you're exporting to .epub, Reedsy, Draft2Digital, and Calibre are excellent, free options that preserve style and formatting without breaking your layout.

Before you click that final "Export" or "Upload" button, do one last read-through—especially of the beginning and ending. Make sure there are no leftover placeholders, missing chapter titles, or weird formatting glitches. Check that your italics carried over, your paragraph breaks stayed consistent, and your header/footer didn't vanish.

It's also a good idea to preview your manuscript in multiple formats. Open your PDF and scroll through on your phone, your tablet, or your Kindle app. Catch anything that looks off—extra spacing, a bold heading that shouldn't be bold, an indent that's gone missing. This step makes your story feel real and shows you what your readers will experience.

If you're publishing in paperback or hardcover, formatting becomes more advanced. Page numbers, trim size, margins, gutters, and justification all matter. You might consider using a dedicated tool like Vellum (Mac only), Atticus, or hiring a formatter. But even if you're doing it yourself, ChatGPT can guide you through the requirements: "What are the ideal page margins for a 6x9 paperback book on Amazon KDP?" and it'll walk you through the math.

When it's all done—when your book is formatted, clean, exported, and saved in multiple formats—you've crossed the last mile of the race. You've turned an idea, sparked in a single day, into a manuscript that looks ready to sit on a shelf, be held in a hand, and make a real impression.

This part of the process isn't glamorous. It doesn't come with the adrenaline of writing a twist or the emotional thrill of a satisfying ending. But it's where you show the world that you care. That your work deserves to be taken seriously. That your one-day novel *isn't* a rushed mess—it's a real book, built with vision, voice, and respect for the reader.

So export it clean. Format it right. Make it shine. And then move forward knowing your story looks as good as it reads.

Cover Design and Titles with AI Input

You've got a completed manuscript, polished and formatted, and now it's time to put a face on it. Literally. The cover of your book is the first impression it makes on a reader, whether they're scrolling through Amazon listings or glancing at a social media ad. It needs to tell them what kind of story they're getting, what tone to expect, and why they should care. And right next to that cover is your title—the handful of words that either grabs a reader by the collar or disappears into the noise. Luckily, you don't have to figure it all out on your own. AI, including ChatGPT and image-generation tools, can help you design an eye-catching cover and brainstorm the perfect title that fits your story's soul.

Let's start with the **title**, because it shapes your cover design and marketing strategy. A good title isn't just catchy—it's aligned with your genre, your tone, and your intended audience. A thriller title like *The Final Witness* says something different than a romance title like *Hearts on Fire* or a fantasy title like *The Bone Prophet*. If your AI-written story came together quickly, you might not have had time to dwell on title possibilities. That's where ChatGPT comes in.

Tell it everything: your story's plot, themes, mood, target genre, and what kind of emotional response you want the title to evoke. Then ask, "Can you give me ten original title ideas for this story?" Better yet, get specific: "Give me ten title options for a dark mystery about a grieving detective who discovers a conspiracy inside his own department. Titles should sound ominous and literary." You'll get a list that ranges from poetic to punchy, and often just seeing the options will trigger your own intuition. Even if none are perfect, you'll likely find one you can tweak into something that feels just right.

You can also ask for help with **subtitle ideas** or **series names**. For example: "Suggest a subtitle for *The Silver Memory* that gives it more suspense and market appeal," or "What's a good name for a dystopian trilogy about environmental collapse and rebellion?" ChatGPT can reverse-engineer titles based on marketing logic, genre signals, and reader psychology. Use it.

Once your title is locked in, you're ready to design the **cover**. Even if you don't have a design background, AI image tools like DALL·E, Midjourney, or Canva's Magic Design feature can give you a strong visual starting point. The key is understanding your genre's visual language. A romantic comedy usually features bold fonts, pastel palettes, and character illustrations. A horror novel leans toward high-contrast images, shadows, or creepy typography. A science fiction story might feature futuristic landscapes, spacecraft, or abstract elements.

If you're not sure what visual style fits your book, ask ChatGPT: "What are the most common cover design elements for indie thrillers?" or "Describe a fantasy book cover layout that would appeal to fans of *The Witcher*." You'll get a breakdown of common visual tropes—colors, imagery, font styles—that you can apply to your own design or brief to a designer.

If you're using DALL·E, for example, you can give it a prompt like:

"A dark, moody forest at twilight, with an abandoned cabin in the distance and a mysterious figure in a trench coat standing at the edge. Soft fog, high contrast. Book cover style, cinematic lighting."

That will generate a visual starting point. You can also refine the prompt until you get something closer to your mental image. Once you've got a base image, import it into a design tool like Canva or Photoshop and overlay your title, author name, and any subtitle or tagline.

ChatGPT can even help with **tagline creation**. Ask: "What's a compelling tagline for a psychological thriller about memory loss and betrayal?" or "Give me ten one-line taglines that would hook readers of paranormal romance." These lines can be used on your cover, in your Amazon description, on social media, or as the punchline in your elevator pitch.

If you're on a tight budget, tools like Canva offer templates you can edit with your image and title, or you can use free book cover makers like BookBrush. Ask ChatGPT, "What's the best free online tool for designing a professional eBook cover?" and it'll point you to platforms with no design experience required.

If you're going to hire a designer, ChatGPT can help you write the perfect brief:

"Write a design brief for a freelance book cover designer. The book is a noir crime thriller titled *Crimson Hour*, featuring a morally conflicted private investigator and set in 1950s Chicago. The tone is dark, gritty, and tragic."

This way, your designer has clarity from the start, and you don't have to stumble through explaining your vision.

As you finalize your cover, always preview it in thumbnail size. That's how most readers will first see it—on a website, a phone screen, or in a crowded search result. Ask yourself: is it legible? Is it striking? Does it stand out? ChatGPT can give you a checklist for what makes a good thumbnail-sized cover if you want a second opinion.

The same goes for your title. Plug your top choices into Amazon or Google and see what comes up. Is it unique enough to own? Is it already taken by five other novels in your genre? ChatGPT can also help with that: "Check if the title *Silent Ashes* is commonly used in published fiction." It won't do a full trademark search, but it'll give you a sense of how crowded the name space is.

Once your title and cover are ready, your book finally feels *real*. And here's the beauty of it all—you did it in one day, but it won't look like it. Thanks to a smart partnership with AI, your book will stand side by side with stories that took months or years to complete, and readers won't know the difference. All they'll see is a title that grabs them, a cover that speaks to them, and—once they open the first page—a story that pulls them in.

That's the goal. And with the right tools and a creative eye, you've got everything you need to make it happen.

Getting Feedback and Making Adjustments

You've written the book. You've edited it, formatted it, titled it, and even designed a killer cover. But before you release it into the world—whether that's on a self-publishing platform, in the inbox of a literary agent, or into the hands of beta readers—it's time for one final, crucial step: getting feedback and making smart, focused adjustments. Because no matter how fast you wrote it, or how confident you feel about it, every story benefits from an outside perspective. And that feedback doesn't have to crush your confidence. In fact, if approached the right way, it can fuel your final rewrite and help elevate your book from "done" to *ready*.

Let's start with a mindset shift. Feedback isn't criticism—it's collaboration. It's a chance to see your story from the eyes of a fresh reader, someone who doesn't know what's in your head and only has the words on the page to guide them. And when you've written a novel in a single day, there are bound to be blind spots—moments where something made perfect sense to you but left the reader puzzled, disconnected, or unconvinced. That's not a failure. That's just part of the process.

Your first step is to **decide who you want feedback from**. You don't need a professional editor right away. In fact, for your first round, trusted beta readers are often better. These could be friends, writing group members, fellow indie authors, or even AI itself. You want readers who are honest, kind, and preferably fans of your genre. Let them know you're not looking for praise—you're looking for clarity. Where did they feel engaged? Where did they lose interest? Where did they get confused, bored, or distracted?

Give them a short guide to help them respond. Something like:

- What scenes or chapters did you love?
- Were there any parts you wanted to skip?
- Did you understand what the characters were feeling and why?
- Did anything feel forced, rushed, or unbelievable?
- Was the ending satisfying?

You can also ask for **specific feedback** if you already know where you feel uncertain. "I'm not sure if Chapter 12 feels emotionally strong enough" or "Do you believe the main character's motivation by the end?" Being targeted makes it easier for your readers to help without feeling overwhelmed.

If you don't have beta readers handy, ChatGPT can act as a **stand-in critique partner**. Paste in a chapter or scene and ask, "From a reader's perspective, where might this section lose impact?" or "Are the character emotions in this moment coming through clearly?" AI can't replace a human's gut reaction, but it's surprisingly helpful at highlighting places where your pacing, clarity, or tone may be slipping.

Once you get feedback, it's time to **filter it**. Not all suggestions will align with your vision, and that's okay. Your job is to look for *patterns*. If three different readers point out that the middle feels slow, or that the love interest disappears for too long, that's a signal. If one person didn't like a twist and everyone else loved it, you might choose to keep it. Use your instinct to decide what feels true to the story you're trying to tell.

Now comes the **adjustment phase**, and this is where ChatGPT really shines. Take a note like, "This chapter felt too slow," and feed that into a prompt: "Speed up the pacing in this chapter while keeping the same plot points intact." Or,

"Readers found this character arc unclear. Rewrite this scene to better show the internal conflict." You're not starting over—you're tweaking with intention.

You can also use feedback to polish language. If someone says the dialogue felt stiff, ask ChatGPT, "Rewrite this exchange to sound more natural, like two friends with a tense history." If they felt confused about world rules or stakes, ask, "Add a brief explanation earlier in the story to clarify the fantasy rules without heavy exposition."

The beauty of working with AI is that you can revise quickly and iteratively. Try one version. Read it aloud. Tweak. Try another. You can test three variations of a scene in under thirty minutes. That kind of speed means your revisions stay fresh—you're still emotionally connected to the story while improving it.

As you apply changes, keep checking back in with your **core vision**. Ask yourself: does this still feel like *my* book? Do the changes improve clarity and flow without diluting the story's voice or emotional truth? If you start to feel like you're editing just to please someone else, pause. You want feedback to make your book better—not to make it someone else's book.

And remember, "better" doesn't mean "perfect." The goal isn't to eliminate all imperfections. It's to sharpen what's working, fix what's confusing, and make sure the story lands the way *you* intended. If the ending makes people cry in a good way, or the twist makes them gasp, or the main character feels real and raw, you've done your job.

Once you've made your adjustments, do a final pass. Read through the book one last time—ideally out loud or with a text-to-speech tool—to make sure the flow still feels strong and your edits haven't introduced any new issues. Look for leftover typos, awkward transitions, or places where the pacing hiccups after a rewrite.

Then—congratulate yourself. You wrote a book in a day. You revised it with focus. You accepted feedback with grace. And now you've polished it into something ready for the world. That's not just writing. That's *authoring*.

The final step? Hit publish. Or send that query. Or hold your book in your hands, proud of every line. You didn't just write fast—you wrote smart. And you gave your story the care it deserved, even on a wild timeline. That's how great books happen. One honest draft, one bit of feedback, and one brave adjustment at a time.

The Joy of Finishing a Fiction Book in One Day

There's a unique, electric kind of joy that comes from finishing a fiction book in one day. It's a mix of exhaustion and elation, disbelief and pride, the kind of quiet triumph that makes you look at the blinking cursor at the end of the final sentence and think, *Did I really just do that?* And yes, you did. You took an idea from spark to story, shaped characters, moved them through conflict and growth, built worlds, wrote dialogue, crafted tension—and you did it all in a single stretch of time, with ChatGPT riding shotgun, helping you pull the pieces together.

It's not just about speed. It's about momentum. Focus. Flow. It's about trusting your gut and letting the words lead you, sentence after sentence, until the shape of something real starts to take form on the screen. Writing an entire book in a day is an act of commitment. It's diving in without fear, knowing that the story might twist and tangle, but you'll follow it anyway. It's letting go of perfection and embracing progress. And when you reach the end—whether it took six hours or sixteen—it feels like magic.

There's joy in the *freedom* of it. When you write fast, you silence the inner critic. You don't have time to second-guess or self-edit every word. You're not stuck analyzing whether a metaphor is too much or if the pacing is off. You're just writing. Creating. Breathing life into something that didn't exist that morning. And that freedom can unlock a voice you didn't know you had. A sharper instinct. A braver idea. A deeper truth.

There's joy in the *surprises*, too. When you write without overplanning, you give your story space to surprise you. Maybe a character said something you didn't expect. Maybe a subplot appeared out of nowhere and just worked. Maybe the ending wrote itself and gave you chills. That's the thrill of writing fast with intuition guiding the wheel—your conscious mind steps aside, and your storytelling instinct takes over. And when it happens, it's better than caffeine.

And let's not overlook the joy of *completion*. So many writers start books they never finish. Pages stack up, then stall. Ideas fade. Stories get abandoned. But not this time. This time, you finished. You saw it through. It's done. That feeling of finality is like exhaling after holding your breath. It's one thing to imagine a story. It's another to live inside it and come out the other side with a full manuscript. Whether it's rough or polished, short or epic—it's a book. And it's yours.

Writing with ChatGPT doesn't lessen the achievement. It amplifies it. You still made every decision. You still felt your way through every scene. You were the director, the navigator, the architect of meaning. ChatGPT was a tool—a fast, responsive, idea-sparking tool—but the story is still powered by your vision. And the speed doesn't cheapen the work. It proves that with focus and the right support, we can do far more than we often allow ourselves to believe.

Then there's the *physical joy* of being done. The stretch of your arms. The sigh of your back leaving the chair. The thrill of seeing a complete story on your screen, knowing that a day ago it didn't exist. Maybe you print it out. Maybe you save it in a folder called "Completed." Maybe you just sit there smiling at the screen, reading that last line one more time. It's real now. Tangible. A finished story, written in a single creative blaze.

And you didn't just write a book. You rewired your belief about what's possible. You proved to yourself that you can do something big, something bold, something creative—and you can do it *now*, not someday. That belief stays with you. It changes how you approach every future writing project. It removes the fear of the blank page. It gives you confidence to start again, anytime, anywhere.

Even if the book isn't perfect—and it won't be—it's yours to shape. You can revise it, expand it, tighten it, publish it. Or you can let it stand as a monument to what you're capable of in one day. Either way, you've captured something rare. Not just a story, but a moment. A day where you made space for creativity and chased it all the way to the end.

So take a moment. Celebrate. Share your success with someone who'll cheer you on. Say the words: "I wrote a book today." Because you did. And not many people can say that.

Tomorrow, you can return to the slower pace if you want. You can tweak and polish and plan and refine. But today, you did something extraordinary. You showed up, locked in, and created a world from scratch.

That's the joy of finishing a fiction book in one day.

That's the joy of being a writer.

Prompting Like a Pro – Getting the Best Responses from ChatGPT

The secret to unlocking the full creative potential of ChatGPT lies in the prompt. A vague prompt gives you generic output. A great prompt, though—one that's rich, clear, and specific—can deliver incredibly detailed, original, and imaginative content. This chapter is about turning you into a master of the prompt. If you want your one-day novel to shine, you need ChatGPT to work with precision and depth. That all starts with knowing exactly what to ask.

Let's walk through some examples that will help you generate gold for six essential aspects of your fiction writing: story ideas, character development, world building, settings, plot structure, and working with the end in mind.

1. Story Ideas

A weak prompt:

"Give me a story idea."

Sure, ChatGPT will respond. But you'll get something vague, maybe even cliché.

A great prompt:

"Give me 3 original story ideas for a mystery novel where the detective is blind, set in a small coastal town, and the murder connects to something buried in the town's history. Keep the tone dark and literary."

This gives the AI clarity, direction, and tone. You'll get highly specific, intriguing ideas that you can use immediately or adapt further.

Another example:

"Pitch me a science fiction story idea involving time travel, a protagonist who is trying to prevent their younger self from making a world-ending mistake, and a government agency that controls memory."

Now you're giving genre, premise, emotional hook, and a twist. You'll get something bold and usable.

2. Character Development

A weak prompt:

"Describe a character for my novel."

You'll get a basic sketch.

A great prompt:

"Create a female protagonist in her 30s who is an ex-opera singer turned private investigator. She's emotionally guarded, has a deep secret tied to her past on stage, and drinks too much coffee. Give me her backstory, strengths, flaws, and a unique habit she has when she's nervous."

That kind of detail opens the door to layered, memorable characters.

You can also ask:

"What would motivate a young priest to become a contract killer while still believing in God? Build me this character's moral journey and internal conflict."

Now you're asking for emotional complexity. The response you get will often surprise you in the best way.

3. World Building

A weak prompt:

"Make up a fantasy world."

Generic fantasy tropes will appear.

A strong prompt:

"Create a fantasy world where all power is derived from music, and only those who can hear a certain frequency can access magic. Describe the geography, the social structure, the ruling class, and the secret history that was buried after a failed revolution."

This leads to a rich world you can build a whole novel around.

Or try this:

"Describe a dystopian Earth where the oceans have turned to thick sludge, and humanity now lives in airborne cities powered by algae. Include cultural traditions, political systems, and the struggles of the lower classes."

Now you've got setting, atmosphere, and theme all rolled into one.

4. Settings

A weak prompt:

"Describe a setting for my book."

Okay, but what kind of book?

A great prompt:

"Describe a decaying Victorian manor in the English countryside where the final scene of a gothic horror novel takes place. It should feel unsettling but beautiful. Mention details like scent, lighting, and sound."

The setting becomes cinematic, not just background.

Another powerful one:

"Give me the description of a bustling, futuristic market on Mars where illegal tech is sold and secrets change hands. Focus on the colors, sounds, and smells."

You'll get immersive, sensory details that drop the reader into your world immediately.

5. Plot Structure

A weak prompt:

"What should happen in my story?"

Not helpful.

A great prompt:

"Outline a three-act structure for a romantic thriller where a woman discovers her husband is not who he says he is, and the truth puts both of their lives in danger. Start with the ending in mind: he dies trying to protect her from the people he betrayed. Include major beats for Acts 1, 2, and 3."

That gives you a complete roadmap.

You can also ask:

"Create a plot outline for a comedy about a struggling actor who impersonates a famous psychologist on live TV, and suddenly becomes a national sensation. The climax should involve him being exposed in the most public way possible."

You'll get a tight, scene-by-scene blueprint to write from.

6. Working with the End in Mind

A weak prompt:

"How should my story end?"

That's open-ended in the wrong way.

A better approach:

"I want my story to end with the protagonist sacrificing their chance at love to save their sibling from prison. What could be a fitting beginning and midpoint that make this ending feel inevitable yet heartbreaking?"

Now you're asking for thematic resonance and emotional payoff.

Another approach:

"Here's my ending: a young woman turns herself in for a crime she didn't commit to protect the real culprit—her sister. What is a compelling opening chapter and inciting incident that set this up?"

This leads to a novel that feels intentional, structured, and satisfying from start to finish.

The magic formula here is **specificity + intent = quality output**. Give ChatGPT a clear job, a little emotion, and a touch of direction—and you'll get answers that push your story further than you thought possible.

Master your prompts, and you'll master the page. In one day or any day.

Creating Prompts That Enhance and Continue Your Story

When you're writing a fiction book in one day with ChatGPT, the secret to keeping the story flowing is asking the right questions at the right time. You're not just writing—you're co-creating with an AI that's waiting for your direction. And to keep that collaboration dynamic, emotionally engaging, and narratively consistent, you need to craft prompts that don't just generate content—they *enhance* the storytelling and *continue* the momentum. You're not just feeding ChatGPT random ideas; you're giving it clear paths to walk down, and sometimes, pushing it to dig deeper.

One of the most important things to understand is that you don't have to think in terms of big plot leaps every time. Small, smart prompts can carry you through a story with nuance and emotional continuity. For example, if you've just written a tense scene between two characters and need to keep the emotional rhythm intact, you might say, "Continue this scene but focus on what each character is feeling internally, even if they don't say it aloud." That's a simple prompt, but it gives ChatGPT a new lens through which to keep the scene alive without forcing a shift in tone or location.

Sometimes, the story pauses because you're unsure what should happen next. That's the perfect moment for a prompt like, "What are three possible directions this scene could go in that stay true to the protagonist's goal but add new tension?" This doesn't just continue the story—it opens doors you might not have seen. And it keeps the development aligned with the character's trajectory rather than throwing in a random twist that doesn't feel earned.

You can also use prompts to reframe the moment you're in. Let's say the pacing feels flat. Instead of continuing the story in a straight line, try: "What's a surprising but believable complication that could happen right now, raising the stakes without introducing a new character?" Or: "Describe this next chapter from a secondary character's perspective to reveal something the protagonist doesn't know yet." These kinds of prompts enhance what you've already written and deepen the narrative layers while still moving forward.

Dialogue can also benefit from smart continuation prompts. If you want a conversation to evolve, don't just say, "Write more dialogue." Try: "Continue this argument, but let both characters reveal something personal they hadn't intended to say." That adds emotional weight, keeps the reader hooked, and shows character development—without having to stop the flow or rewrite the scene entirely.

You can also use prompts to maintain continuity. If you're twenty chapters in and not sure how to bring things full circle, ask: "Based on everything we've written so far, what unresolved threads need closure, and how could we start weaving them into the final chapters?" ChatGPT will scan the themes and moments you've mentioned and help build a satisfying finish that feels intentional, not rushed.

Sometimes the story just needs a little boost in energy or mood. For that, you can use style-driven prompts like, "Continue the next scene in the tone of a suspenseful thriller, but keep the character dynamics intact," or "Add a layer of dark humor to this next scene while still progressing the plot." You're not just asking for more—you're asking for *more with flavor*.

You can also guide the AI to reinforce the story's deeper meaning. If your book is about identity, loss, or redemption, prompt the AI with, "Write the next scene in a way that subtly echoes the story's theme of [insert theme], without being obvious." This encourages subtext, symbolism, and emotional resonance—all things that lift a story from good to great.

The goal is to keep the writing responsive and intentional, not mechanical. You're not just extending word count—you're continuing the emotional, narrative, and thematic current you've started. And the more clearly your prompt captures that goal, the better the AI can deliver something useful, exciting, and creatively aligned with your vision.

So next time you hit that blinking cursor and wonder, *what now?*, don't just ask for "the next scene." Ask for the next scene that *matters*. Prompt with emotion. With conflict. With purpose. The story will keep moving—not because you're forcing it to, but because you're feeding it the right questions.

When you prompt with curiosity and intention, the novel doesn't just continue—it evolves. And that's how you keep writing forward, even when the day is long and the story's still unfolding.

Good luck with your next project. I hope you liked this book, if you did please leave a review where you bought it. Thank you from the author.

www.ingramcontent.com/pod-product-compliance
Lightning Source LLC
LaVergne TN
LVHW082350200926
848481LV00012B/3523